❧ F A B U L O U S ❧
FLOORCLOTHS
create contemporary floor coverings from an old world art

Caroline O'Neill Kuchinsky

The entry hall of Homewood House in Baltimore, Maryland, showcases a spectacular fitted floorcloth in the "Running Diamond" pattern. (Courtesy Homewood House Museum, The Johns Hopkins University.)

Published by

 krause publications

700 East State St., Iola, WI 54990-0001
Telephone 715-445-2214
www.krause.com

Please call or write for our free catalog of
publications. Our toll-free number to place an
order or obtain a free catalog is 800-258-0929 or
please use our regular business telephone
715-445-2214.

Illustrations by Golden Dog Productions
Photography by Barbara Hunt Photography
Designed by Jan Wojtech
Manufactured in the United States of America

Library of Congress Cataloging-in-Publication
Data

Kuchinsky, Caroline O'Neill
        Fabulous floorcloths: create contemporary floor coverings from an
old world art

        p. 128

        ISBN 0-8019-9054-8

        1. Floorcloths   2. Crafts   3. Floor coverings

                                    97-69814
                                    CIP

Dedication

I would like to dedicate this book to my husband Michael and my children, Isobel, Rachel, and Louis. Without them this book would still be a dream and not a reality.

Acknowledgments

I would like to express my immense gratitude to the people, places, and companies who helped to create this book:

Barbara Case, my editor, for her guidance and experience in the publishing field.

John Riina, my agent, whose experience, advice, and willingness to work with me is greatly appreciated.

Bonnie Fatigati, my illustrator, who created fabulous artwork and helped me more than she'll ever know.

Barbara Hunt, my photographer, whose skill and patience made this a great book and a photographic learning experience.

Homewood House Museum and Rosanna Moore for sharing their beautiful floorcloths and knowledge.

Fredrix Artist Canvas for supplying the canvas for the floorcloth projects in the book.

The Gaithersburg Paint Center and Benjamin Moore & Co. for supplying the paint and protective sealers for the floorcloth projects.

DecoArt for supplying their Americana Acrylics paint.

Plaid Enterprises for supplying their Decorator Block stamps, Mod Podge glue, and stencils.

Hoffman Fabrics for the use of their "Windsor" fabric.

Amscan, Inc. for their "Classic Scroll" luncheon napkin.

Mafcote Industries, Inc. and Royal Lace for their "Basket Lace Square" doily.

Concord Fabrics for their "Seed Packet" fabric.

Alexander Henry Fabrics, Inc. for their "In the Beginning" fabric.

Imperial Wallcoverings, Inc. for their "Scroll" wallpaper border.

Ruby Hough and Donna O'Neill for their design and color expertise.

My sister Kathleen for her help and support no matter the time of day.

Michael, John, and Cindy O'Neill, and Katherine, Joe, and Bill Kuchinsky for their patience and support.

My mother and father for inspiring me to work hard, succeed, and follow my dreams.

My mother for her endless support, love, and limitless help.

Finally, my husband Michael for believing in me and the finished book. Thank you.

FABULOUS FLOORCLOTHS
CONTENTS

Introduction

SECTION I: GETTING STARTED

Chapter 1: Selecting a Design & Color Scheme

Questions to Consider, Decisions to Make . 5
Selecting a Design 5
Choosing a Color Scheme 6
Patterns & Textures. 8
Making Floorcloth Samples 8

Chapter 2: Materials

General Materials & Tools 11
Decorative Mediums 14

Chapter 3: Basic Floorcloth Construction & Care

Cutting & Stretching the Canvas 17
Preparing & Basecoating the Canvas 18
Enlarging & Transferring the Design 19
Sealing Your Floorcloth 21
Hemming the Edges. 22
Caring for Your Floorcloth 26

Chapter 4: Decorating Your Floorcloth

Freehand Painting 28
    Lattice 28
    Crescents 29
    Puzzle Painting. 30
    Swirls, Curls & Waves 31
Borders 31
    Solid Borders 32
    Checkered Borders 33
    Freehand Fringe & Roping. 34

◆◆ Stencils, Stamps & Patterns 36
    Stamping 37
    Bricks 39
    Ferns 40
    Doily Spray 40
Faux Finishes 41
    Sponge Painting 42
    Color Washing 44
    Veining 44

Chapter 5: Other Embellishments

Paper Decoupage 48
    Decoupage Cutouts 49
    Decoupage Borders 51
    Paper Napkins & Tissue Paper 53
Fabric Appliqué 55

SECTION II: PROJECTS

Chapter 6: Simple Floorcloth Projects

Ornamental Tile 60
Swirls, Curls & Waves 64
Circle of Stars 66
Contemporary Crescents 70
Fruits & Flowers 73
Rainbow Hopscotch 76
Classical Table Runner 79

Chapter 7: Intermediate Floorcloth Projects

Garden View 84
White & Black Marble 87
Welcome Home 92
Victorian Lace 96

Chapter 8: Advanced Floorcloth Projects

Stained Glass 100
Animal Escapades 104
Lattice & Fringe 109
Santa Fe 113

About the Author 118
Suppliers 119
Selected Reading 120
Index 121

Introduction

Would you like to transform an ordinary floor in your home into a work of art without hiring a professional decorator or spending a lot of money? It's easier than you think. You can create a one-of-a-kind canvas floorcloth exactly the right size to fit your room in exactly the right colors for your decor. Whether you are a novice crafter or an experienced artist, you can create a floorcloth to use and enjoy for years to come.

Also known as an oil cloth, wax cloth, or painted rug, a floorcloth is simply a piece of canvas cut and hemmed to any size. You can paint, embellish, and varnish it to create an ornamental yet highly durable and functional floor covering that will add new patterns, colors, and textures to your room.

Floorcloth popularity began during the early 18th century in Europe and crossed the ocean to America a few years later. Imported from Britain, where floorcloth production was already underway, floorcloths were purchased by wealthy Americans or made by novice crafters. Often the canvases were painted to resemble marble or painted floors using stencils, freehand designs, or block prints. In more affluent homes, the floorcloths were laid over expensive carpets as crumb catchers.

As the American economy prospered and general manufacturing developed, so did the production of floorcloths. The American Revolution was a turning point in floorcloth making. For the first time, materials were produced in America and the art form began to rival that of Britain. Floorcloths were soon found in less affluent households, often covering a floor of unfinished wood planks or dirt.

It wasn't until the late 1900s that floorcloth popularity began to dwindle,

A lady's dressing room in Maryland's Homewood House features a geometric patterned floorcloth. The design is a variation of John Carwitham's plate #11 from Various Kinds of Floorcloths, 1739. (Courtesy Homewood House Museum, The John Hopkins University.)

ultimately being overshadowed by the new "linoleum."

In the last decade, floorcloths have enjoyed a resurgence of popularity, and for good reason. Today, more than ever, we want our homes to be a reflection of our personal tastes and pleasures. What better way than to create our own art to decorate our homes? Today, floorcloths aren't limited to Colonial or early American designs. Myriad patterns and motifs can be incorporated to blend with any decorating style and modern painting techniques, products, and decorative applications open up a host of possibilities for the making of this rejuvenated art form.

With this book you will learn how to design and create professional looking floorcloths. **Section I: Getting Started** shows how to choose designs and color schemes to fit any decorating style. You'll learn about materials, tools, and decorative mediums and the step-by-step illustrations will guide you through the basic techniques for floorcloth construction and care. You'll explore different ways to decorate your floorcloth, including painted applications and embellishing techniques such as stenciling, border painting, fringe, lattice, doily spray, stamping and veining, paper decoupage, and fabric appliqué.

Section II: Projects provides instructions for 15 exciting and unique floorcloth projects. The projects are divided into Simple, Intermediate, and Advanced, or you can mix and match techniques to create your own personalized design.

I hope this book provides you with the instruction and inspiration to make many floorcloths to enjoy in your home for years to come.

Caroline O'Neill Kuchinsky

SECTION 1: GETTING STARTED

CHAPTER 1:
SELECTING A DESIGN & COLOR SCHEME

QUESTIONS TO CONSIDER, DECISIONS TO MAKE

Selecting a design and color scheme is one of the most enjoyable steps in the process of making your floorcloth, but it can also be a bit overwhelming. Weeding out your choices to find the perfect design takes a bit of time, thought, and planning. I have found that planning is the key to creating any beautiful and long lasting work of art.

First consider the amount of time and artistic experience you have. The amount of time you can devote to making the floorcloth will help you narrow down the design choices. If you choose a design from the advanced project list, you'll need to commit more time to it than a simpler project would require. If you're not familiar with a technique, you'll need extra time to practice and master it. This isn't meant to discourage you from trying a challenging project, but to prepare you for the time commitment. Because of this, you may want to begin with a simple project, then move on to a more complex one.

Also consider the size and design of the floorcloth you want to make. Large floorcloths take more time and effort to complete; some designs are quite simple and require little work, while other more complex designs require additional time and effort.

SELECTING A DESIGN

The variety of decorative applications in this book have been purposely selected so you can create simple, complex, or elaborate designs in a short period of time. No matter what decorative style you prefer, the design possibilities are numerous. There are many design options presented in these pages, but you can find potential floorcloth designs almost anywhere.

When looking for ideas, remember to keep in mind your time frame, artistic ability, and the floorcloth size. Carry a small notebook and jot down ideas that appeal to you. If you plan to make a floorcloth for a specific room, the design and color scheme should relate to the furnishings in the room. You can coordinate your floorcloth design with the decorating style of the room or choose a different style to complement the room and add a more versatile feel to its decor.

Don't overlook accessories when searching for the perfect design. Wall coverings, the fabric on pillows and drapes, other floor coverings, tableware, artwork, or even a set of sheets, can provide inspiration.

Architecture is another source for interesting ideas, whether it be real buildings, photos, or drawings from books. You'll find a host of books at the library pertaining to different styles and periods of architecture. Many architectural details and motifs such as moldings, columns, and friezes can be used in combination to create decorative borders and center motifs for a floorcloth.

I find many designs in ornamental design books which are divided into different periods of historical design with detailed explanations of patterns, motifs, color schemes, and their origins. The color plates are extremely helpful when designing a reproduction or stylized floorcloth from a certain era. This eliminates any guesswork when selecting a color scheme and saves valuable working time.

If you own a computer, you can purchase software programs with large selections of "clip art" which can help in creating your design.

Magazines and catalogs are other good sources for ideas and designs. Photos and other artwork can be cut out and decoupaged to the canvas. When you see a design that appeals to you, keep it, even if it's not related to your current project. This is an easy and fun way to build a library of ideas for future projects.

CHOOSING A COLOR SCHEME

The color scheme you choose will determine whether the floorcloth will unobtrusively blend into your decor or become a focal point of the room. Do you want a bright and bold floor covering or something subtle and muted? Should the design stand out from the background or blend in? The colors you choose for the background and the design will make a big difference in the intensity of the design. It's a good idea to make several small floorcloth samples in different color combinations to see how the colors affect the design.

Make selecting a design and choosing a color scheme easier by creating a small floorcloth sample of each design idea.

Understanding color is easier than you think. Perhaps you are one of those lucky people who has the ability to choose colors easily. If not, a little reading and a bit of hands-on experience is all you need to become more comfortable with this part of the project.

To understand how a successful color scheme works, it is important to learn how colors work together. Are the colors bright and bold or muted and soft?

Bright and Bold Colors

1-1

Muted and Soft Colors

To help you understand color, collect a variety of paint chips from your local paint store. Cut apart the chips and mix and match colors in different combinations to see how different colors work together. Then purchase some inexpensive water-based acrylic paints and poster board and experiment with color combinations. Put dark green next to peach, then next to dark blue. You'll soon see how colors work individually and together as a whole. By experimenting with the paint samples, you will discover that a color changes according to the circumstances under which it is viewed (Figure 1-2). The red in the diagram appears to be slightly lighter and less intense on the dark background than when shown against a lighter taupe background.

Dark colors visually shrink the working space of the floorcloth and make it seem smaller, while light colors visually open the space and make it seem larger.

1-2

Although it's tempting to choose color schemes that are currently in style, try to avoid this route unless they coordinate with the room you're decorating. The life span of a popular color scheme is quite limited and by the time you've designed and finished your floorcloth, a trendy color scheme may be out of style.

Instead, select colors that reflect your own taste and complement your decor. Set the room's tone with color. Will it be soft and subtle, bright and lively, or somewhere in between? Color schemes associated with particular decorating periods are timeless, but the *shades* of each color often change from one year to the next. When in doubt, check decorator books and magazines for the particular period or style you are interested in and incorporate it into your floorcloth design.

Continue your color education by studying the area where the floorcloth will be placed. Note the different colors in the room to get a starting palette of colors to work from. Look for color ideas in other items in

your home such as clothes, furniture, and accessories. Fabric is always an excellent place to find color schemes, since the work of matching and choosing the colors has already been done. Try combining several fabrics to create the illusion of pattern and texture. Look to nature for color combinations and patterns that are visually pleasing and coordinated.

If you are unsure about mixing different colors, stay with a monochromatic color scheme—one basic color in varying shades from light to dark (Figure 1-3). For a clean uncluttered effect, choose several neutral shades and an accent color (Figure 1-4).

1-3

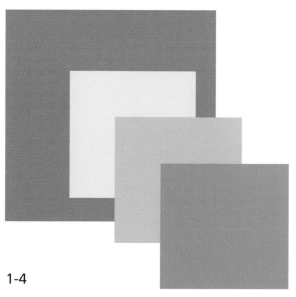

1-4

PATTERNS & TEXTURES

Mixing bold patterns and subtle textures adds dimension and interest to the overall appearance of a floorcloth.

Patterns and textures play an important role in the overall design of your floorcloth. Patterns can be natural or man-made and are rarely without some type of texture, whether it be visual or tactile. When you look at something and imagine the way the surface will feel, you've been affected by its *visual texture*. *Tactile texture* is the actual feel of the surface, whether it be rough, smooth, silky, or bumpy.

Think of polished wood next to a nubby carpet or a shiny mirror mounted on a sponge-painted wall. Patterns and textures create movement and in turn create an exciting design. A monochromatic one-color floorcloth with a variety of textures can be as exciting as a multicolored vivid floorcloth with little texture.

Textured paint finishes (sponging, ragging, stippling, stenciling) create a variety of interesting patterns and imprints. The textures will vary in intensity, depending on the color scheme. Before applying even one brush stroke of paint on your floorcloth canvas, practice the technique you've chosen with a variety of color schemes.

MAKING FLOORCLOTH SAMPLES

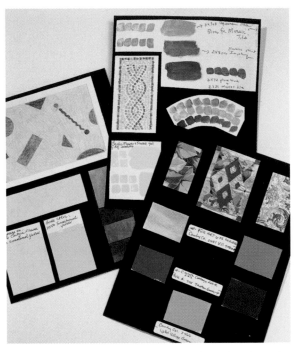

Several floorcloth sample boards showing the initial colored sketch, paint chips, and the decorative applications used.

Making samples is an important and necessary step in the process of creating a successful floorcloth. Regardless of the type of floorcloth you're making, a small-scale sample of each design or a corner view is a good idea for future reference. Samples also help you determine the proportion of each color in relation to the design and show how the colors work together as a whole.

Make small black and white photocopies of the original design and color them with colored pencils or markers. This is a convenient way to test color schemes without having to redraw the design each time. Once you settle on a color scheme, take this to the art supply store to find matching acrylic paints. Make a larger sample and glue it to a piece of poster board.

Make paint swatches of each color and glue these to the poster board as shown in Figure 1-5. Next to each color, write the paint's brand name, color name, style number, and the method you used to apply the color.

CONTEMPORARY CRESCENTS

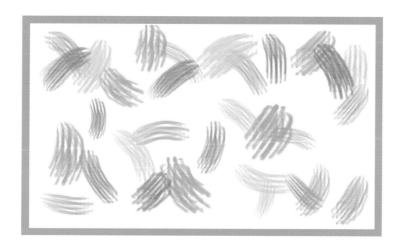

Finished Size: 30″ x 36″
Cut Size: 34″ x 40″

◆ DecoArt, <u>Americana</u>, "Uniform Blue" DA86

◆ DecoArt, <u>Americana</u>, "Colonial Green" DA81

◆ DecoArt, <u>Americana</u>, "French Mauve" DA186

◆ DecoArt, <u>Americana</u>, "Moon Yellow" DA7

◇ Benjamin Moore, <u>MooreGard</u> Low Lustre #01

Description: Solid green border surrounds center of multicolored crescent shapes applied with 1″ and 2″ bristle brushes.

1-5

CHAPTER 2:
MATERIALS

GENERAL MATERIALS & TOOLS

General materials used in making a floorcloth. Top to bottom: primed canvas, artist's stretcher strips, primer, spray paint, corrugated cardboard, foam board, plywood, exterior latex paint, 1" x 2" wood stretchers, wax, acrylic latex varnish.

TYPES OF CANVAS

You can buy canvas either unprimed or primed. The canvas most suitable to use for floorcloths is generally primed with artist's gesso or a universal primer on the front and either primed or unprimed on the back.

Canvas is usually sold by the yard, bolt, or in precut pieces, depending on the type. Generally I use a lightweight canvas for small doormat-size floorcloths and a heavier weight canvas for anything larger.

I use several different primed canvases, depending on the size of the floorcloth I'm making. I like

Fredrix artist's canvas, which is widely available in art supply stores or mail order catalogs. Fredrix sells most of their canvas by style number and name and most types are available by the yard or bolt.

Fredrix "floorcloth" canvas is a heavy cotton duck, double-primed on one side and treated on the back for added strength and durability. Because this type of canvas is sealed on both sides, it doesn't require stretching and can be left unhemmed or hemmed prior to painting and other decorating techniques, thus preventing the canvas from shrinking unevenly. This canvas is available by the bolt and in precut pieces.

Fredrix #123 Dixie is a heavyweight primed 12-ounce canvas suitable for floorcloths four feet or larger. It's available by the yard and bolt. Fredrix #569 Dallas is a medium-weight primed canvas suitable for floorcloths approximately four feet or smaller. It too is available by the yard and bolt. Fredrix Taracloth (sign cloth) is a lightweight triple-coated cotton blend great for place mats, runners, and small (2' x 3') floorcloths where water and moisture are present. Taracloth is available in bolts of three yards to 100 yards.

Unprimed canvas or raw cotton duck is available from art supply stores, canvas suppliers, sail makers, and fabric stores in widths of 60"-120". Some canvas suppliers sell their canvas by number. Numbers 8, 10, and 12 are suitable for floorcoths, with 8 being the heavier weight and 12 being lighter. Most floorcloths are made of 10- or 12-ounce canvas which is stable and heavy enough to withstand everyday wear and tear.

You can also use painter's canvas drop cloths when making large floorcloths, but it tends to shrink a bit more than artist's cotton duck and often has a center seam and/or rubber backing.

When making circular, oblong, or irregularly shaped floorcloths, draw the shape on a square or rectangular piece of canvas so that you can more easily mount and stretch it on a frame. You can cut the shape out just before hemming. For odd shapes, I recommend a canvas such as #569 Dallas. It's easier to hem irregular shapes on a light to medium weight canvas primed on only one side. There's less bulk to contend with than on canvas primed on both sides.

CALCULATING HOW MUCH CANVAS TO BUY

Regardless of the type of canvas you choose, buy enough for the finished floorcloth size plus a minimum of four inches added to the length and width. For example, if the finished size of the floorcloth is 24" x 36," cut the canvas 28" x 40". The additional canvas allows for stretching, shrinking, hemming, and removing the staples.

STRETCHERS & FRAMES

Stretching your canvas is not absolutely necessary, but I strongly recommend it. A stretcher prevents the canvas from shrinking unevenly, buckling, and rippling, and thus lays the groundwork for a smooth professional looking floorcloth. There are two types of frames you can use to stretch your canvas.

For floorcloths 4' x 8' or smaller, you can use a flat frame made of sheet plywood, foam board, corrugated cardboard, or any other sturdy material. This type of frame works best with floorcloth canvas that is already treated and sealed on the back. Secure the canvas to the frame with a staple gun, heavy-duty masking tape, or if using corrugated cardboard, a household stapler. These materials can be purchased at lumber yards, fine art supply stores, and mail order art supply catalogs.

For floorcloths larger than 4' x 8' or canvas that is unprimed or primed only on one side, use open stretcher frames and prepare the canvas by priming it if necessary and adding a non-skid product or sealant on the back.

Open stretcher frames are available in two types. The first type, known as artist's stretcher strips, are precut mitered wood strips sold individually by the inch, available in lengths up to 96". These are available through art and craft supply stores and mail order catalogs.

The second type of stretchers, called furring strip stretchers, are less expensive and are easy to make from 1" x 2" or 1" x 4" pine furring strips fastened together with flat corner braces. A center brace attached with "T" braces is necessary for frames five feet or larger to prevent the frame from sagging. These supplies can be purchased at lumber and hardware stores.

It's easiest to work on canvas stretched on open stretcher frames that are propped vertically against the wall.

PRIMERS

The purpose of priming is to prepare and shrink the canvas before painting. You'll only need to prime canvas if you buy it unprimed.

To prime a canvas, simply brush two coats of artist's gesso or latex wall primer on the front. Both products work well, but the latex wall primer is less expensive. The choice is a matter of personal preference. In situations where the floorcloth will be near water, I recommend applying primer, sealer, or a non-skid product on the back.

CLEAR SEALERS

Sealers are an absolute must to protect your finished floorcloth. You'll find water-based sealers, oil-based sealers, and paste wax (bowling alley wax). Water-based sealers are non-yellowing, fast drying, and provide excellent protection for your floorcloth. They are easy to apply and clean up with soap and water. I generally avoid oil-based sealers because they yellow quite a bit, require a much longer drying period, and clean up with mineral spirits or turpentine. A non-yellowing clear paste wax, such as bowling alley wax, is suitable only for painted floorcloths.

Water-based sealers are sold under several different names: clear sealer, acrylic sealer, water-borne sealer, polyurethane, and clear acrylic varnish to name a few. Buy a sealer that is water-based and non-yellowing in the finish of your choice. You will find a variety of finishes: dull (matte) has no sheen; satin gives off a slight sheen; semi-gloss provides a moderate sheen; and gloss a high sheen. I prefer a dull or satin finish sealer which gives a slight sheen without making the floorcloth too heavy or plastic looking.

I recommend heavier water-based varnishes sold in specialty paint or hardware stores over thin artist varnishes because they provide the floorcloth with added protection.

RUBBER BACKINGS

A non-skid backing is a good idea for floorcloths in bathrooms, kitchens, and foyers where floors might be slippery. Non-skid spray-on or paint-on rubber products are available and provide a good backing. A thin rubber rug or carpet mat can also be placed under a floorcloth, providing the mat is very thin and has little or no texture.

These products are available in flooring, hardware, or art supply stores.

ADHESIVES

There's no one adhesive to use for floorcloths. You'll use different ones for different techniques. For paper decoupage, use Mod Podge, wallpaper border adhesive, or in some instances, white glue. If adding fabric appliqués to canvas, use Mod Podge or fabric glue.

When pattern spraying, use repositionable spray adhesive to temporarily hold the pattern or design on the canvas.

Painter's masking tape or low-tack tape works best for taping borders and securing stencils because it won't pull the paint underneath off when you remove it. Heavy-duty masking tape is great for holding stretched canvases on a flat stretcher as an alternative to a staple gun. No-fray glue, such as Fray Check, prevents fabric from fraying and either rubber cement or a hot glue gun works well for hemming.

TOOLS
PAINT APPLICATORS

Paint brushes come in a variety of shapes and sizes and create different finished effects depending on their quality, bristle content, length, and shape. You will use a combination of house painting brushes, paint rollers, and artist's brushes when making a floorcloth.

House painting bristle brushes, sponge brushes, and rollers work well for painting backgrounds, borders, or large areas of canvas.

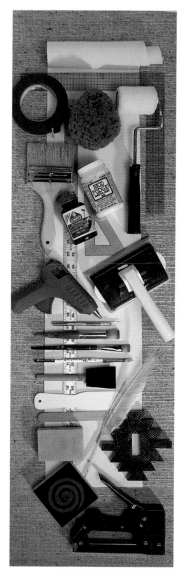

Basic tools for making a floorcloth. Top to bottom: painter's masking tape, natural sea sponge, paint roller, quilter's "L" ruler, bristle paint brush, Mod Podge glue, rubber cement, triangle, hot glue gun, metal yardstick, paint trimmer or pad, craft knife, stencil brush, flat artist's brush, round/pointed artist's brush, sponge paint brush, plastic putty knife, craft stick, undyed feather, kitchen sponge, sponge stamp, rubber stamp, staple gun.

Bristle brushes will have either natural or synthetic bristles. Nylon (synthetic) bristle brushes are good for applying latex paints and natural bristle brushes are good for applying oil-based paints and varnishes. Don't apply varnishes or sealers with a roller, or you'll end up with lots of air bubbles. No matter what type of brush you choose, buy the highest quality bristle brush you can afford—an inexpensive brush may shed bristles and create unwanted brush strokes in the paint.

Sponge brushes and paint pads work well for applying clear sealers. Artist-quality paint brushes work well for applying small amounts of decorative paint to a design. You'll use mostly round, flat, and stencil brushes.

Undyed turkey or duck wing feathers are very effective when painting veining to create marbled finishes. Sponges (natural or synthetic) will help you create a multitude of faux finishes and varying textures.

If you like stamping, you can purchase precut stamps or make your own from rubber, wood, foam, or sponge. These are great for creating repetitive or intricate designs easily and quickly.

Stencils can be purchased precut from mylar, heavy gauge plastic, or metal in a variety of designs or you can make them yourself by cutting a design out of mylar, acetate, or stencil material with a craft knife or electric stencil cutter.

MISCELLANEOUS TOOLS

You'll also need a measuring stick/ruler and a triangle or "L" ruler. Quilting rulers work well because they are transparent and allow you to see your work more clearly. Quilting rulers come in especially handy when drawing in borders and guidelines on the canvas.

For intricate cutting and trimming, you'll need a pair of small scissors and/or a craft knife. For sanding, use fine grade (220 or 320) sandpaper or steel wool and a tack cloth to remove the sanding residue.

Use a craft stick or plastic putty knife to burnish (firmly rub down) tape, paper, or fabric motifs and when folding the edges under for hemming.

DECORATIVE MEDIUMS

When it comes time to decorate your floorcloth, you'll find a wide variety of decorative mediums available. The first decision to make is whether to use water-based or oil-based products.

The projects in this book usually call for water-based products because they are water soluble and dry quickly, allowing you to spend more time working and less time waiting.

A selection of decorative mediums used in making floorcloths. Top to bottom: floral wallpaper border, gold wrapping paper, black and white copies, artist's acrylic paint, paint chips, colored pencils, paint pen, paper napkin, creme stencil paint, floral wrapping paper, craft acrylic paints, color photocopy, 100% cotton decorator fabric, wrapping tissue paper, 100% cotton calico fabric.

It's important to remember that water-based products cannot be applied over oil-based products, but oil-based products can be applied over water-based products.

Whether you choose water-based or oil-based paints, crayons, or markers, you'll get better results by staying with one type throughout the project, because the finished floorcloth will adjust to temperature changes more easily with less chance of cracking paint.

An exception to this rule is the use of oil-based paint pens that are designed to work on any surface.

PAINT

Large areas such as backgrounds can be painted with either latex or alkyd/oil-based paint. Exterior house paint provides the canvas with added flexibility when temperature changes occur. When using latex paint, I recommend a brand with the highest acrylic content possible. The higher the acrylic content, the fewer additives the paint contains and the less the canvas will shrink. You can find high percentages of acrylic in more expensive paint lines, such as Benjamin Moore and Pratt Lambert.

Water-based paint is available in artist-quality acrylics, craft acrylics, gouache, water colors, acrylic sprays, and latex enamels. These paints dry fairly quickly and clean up with water.

Oil-based paint is available in artist-quality oil tubes, crayons, stencil cremes, and alkyd household paints. These paints take longer to dry, especially in high humidity, and clean up with mineral spirits or turpentine.

Water-soluble or impermanent paint (watercolors or gouche, for example) must be sprayed with an artist's fixative to prevent the paint from smearing during the sealing process.

PENS, PENCILS & MARKERS

Paint pens, colored pencils, and markers create interesting and exciting effects. These products can be combined or used individually and are available in permanent and water-soluble finishes. Be sure to check for permanency and spray the canvas with a fixative if necessary before sealing.

PAPER DECOUPAGE

Not all papers work well for decoupage. Those that work best are gift wrap, paper napkins, wrapping tissue paper, wallpaper, and color or black and white photocopies. Stay away from heavier papers such as card stock and calendar paper because they don't adhere well and create unwanted ridges in the floorcloth.

FABRIC APPLIQUÉ

Several types of fabric work well for fabric appliqué. My favorite is 100% cotton calico fabric because it is thin, stable, and easy to handle. Another good choice is 100% polyester because it doesn't shrink and is wafer thin. The heaviest fabric suitable for appliqué is 100% cotton decorator-weight chintz (polished cotton).

Thin fabrics require less sealer than heavier weight fabrics or bulky blends, which can shrink unevenly and bleed. It's best to wash the fabric prior to cutting to remove the sizing and test for color bleeding.

When choosing a patterned fabric, avoid stripes or geometric shapes which can be printed off-grain, making it difficult to glue in a straight line. Instead, choose fabrics with motifs that can be cut out individually, preferably in pieces smaller than eight inches.

CHAPTER 3:
BASIC FLOORCLOTH CONSTRUCTION & CARE

CUTTING & STRETCHING THE CANVAS

The instructions for each floorcloth list the finished size of the floorcloth and the cut size of the canvas, which is four inches wider and longer than the finished size. The additional four inches include a one inch hem for each edge and another inch for stapling and shrinking on each side.

You can cut most canvas with ordinary sharp scissors, but some heavier canvases may require a carpet knife or heavy-duty scissors.

To stretch the canvas, choose the stretcher type that works best for your situation. (Refer to Stretchers and Frames on page 12.) I find it easiest to use an open frame so I can work on both sides of the canvas at the same time. Once the canvas is stretched on the frame, leave it attached until it has been painted, sealed, and cured for several days.

To make a floorcloth larger than 12 feet wide, you may need to combine smaller pieces of canvas. Lay the pieces side by side and tape the seams with wide heavy-duty masking tape and burnish it well. Turn the canvas over and tape the back side of the seams in the same manner. It's best to use unprimed canvas when piecing because the many layers of paint and varnish will build up over the tape and eventually cover and seal the tape edges.

Stretch the canvas on pieces of plywood or foam board to prevent it from buckling. Cover the taped seams with primer or gesso, apply a base coat, decorate, and seal. Primed floorcloth canvas can be used without stretching, but the taped seams will not be covered and sealed as well.

STRETCHING THE CANVAS

MATERIALS

- ∾ Canvas
- ∾ Stretchers and required hardware
- ∾ Staple gun, masking tape, or household stapler for stretching (depends on type of frame)
- ∾ Measuring stick
- ∾ Triangle or "L" ruler
- ∾ Pencil
- ∾ Scissors

❶ Measure and cut the canvas to size (add 4" to the dimensions of the finished floorcloth before cutting).

❷ If using *flat stretchers*, attach the canvas with a household stapler, staple gun, or heavy-duty masking tape, depending on the thickness of the material.

If using *artist's stretchers*, join each mitered corner to form a right angle and insert the wedges provided into the corners to create a tight fit (Figure 3-1).

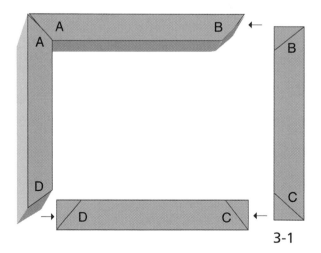

3-1

If using 1" x 2" furring strips, cut the wood strips to match the dimensions of the canvas. Place two stretcher ends perpendicular to each other and join them with a flat corner brace (Figure 3-2). Join the remaining three corners in the same way. For floorcloths five feet and larger, add a center brace to prevent the frame from sagging and secure with two "T" braces.

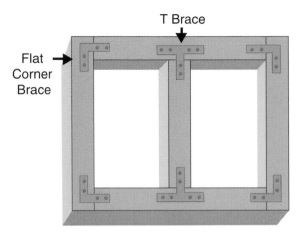

T Brace

Flat Corner Brace

3-2

❸ Open the stretchers. Place the cut canvas, primed side up, on top of the stretcher. Using a staple gun, staple the canvas to the stretcher, with staples 2"-3" apart (Figure 3-3). Start in the middle of each stretcher bar and work to the corners. This stretches the canvas evenly as it is stapled and prevents puckers or ripples.

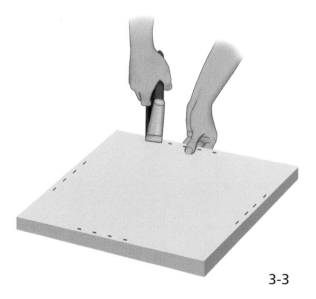

3-3

❹ Continue stapling and stretching to the corners until the entire canvas is secured (Figure 3-4).

3-4

PREPARING & BASECOATING THE CANVAS

MATERIALS

∾ Latex wall primer or artist's gesso (for unprimed canvas only)
∾ Exterior latex wall paint for base coat or background color
∾ Water-based acrylic sealer, varnish, polyurethane, or non-skid rubber backing for back
∾ Short nap paint roller and tray or 4" sponge or nylon bristle paint brush
∾ Measuring stick, triangle, or "L" ruler
∾ Pencil

SECRETS FOR SUCCESS

Use metal rulers and yard sticks. Wood materials are often warped even when new. Be precise when measuring. Dots are more accurate than slash marks.

❶ If using unprimed canvas, apply two coats of latex wall primer or gesso to the front of the canvas with the brush or roller (Figure 3-5). Let dry between coats.

3-5

❷ Turn the frame over and apply a coat of sealer or non-skid backing to the back of the canvas (Figure 3-6). If there's a center brace on the frame, push the canvas away from it to apply the varnish or non-skid backing. Let dry. If you don't want to apply a background color, proceed to Step 4.

3-6

❸ To apply a background color, apply two thin coats of the background paint to the canvas front with a brush or paint roller. Let dry between coats.

❹ Two border lines are necessary to lay out the design. Draw the border lines around the perimeter of the canvas, inside the staples. One line is the *cut line* where the staples are eventually cut away, and the other is the *fold line* where the hem allowance is folded under and glued to the back. It's very important that these lines be straight and the corners are square (90 degree angles). If the lines are at all uneven or crooked, the design and finished floorcloth will be uneven as

well.Using a measuring stick and triangle or "L" ruler, pencil in the cut line around the perimeter of the canvas inside the staples (Figure 3-7). Place a 90 degree triangle in the corners to check that the corners are square and that the opposite sides are equal. Draw the fold line 1" inside the cut line.

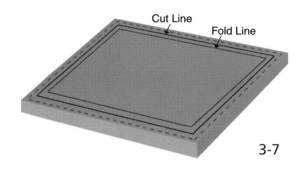

Cut Line
Fold Line

3-7

ENLARGING & TRANSFERRING THE DESIGN

There are a few different ways to enlarge and transfer a design to a canvas. Depending on what equipment is available to you, you can use carbon and graphite paper, graphite shading, visual projectors, photocopy machines, or graph paper.

ENLARGING OR REDUCING

PHOTOCOPY METHOD

❶ Find and mark the center of the design you want to enlarge or reduce (Figure 3-8).

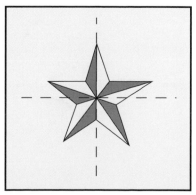

3-8

❷ Enlarge or reduce the design with the % buttons on the copy machine. For example, your drawing's normal size is 100%. To enlarge it twice its size, set the numbers at 200%. To reduce the design by half its size, set the numbers at 50%. When you're enlarging, only part of the design will fit on the copy machine paper, so you'll need to make a copy of each section of the design (Figure 3-9).

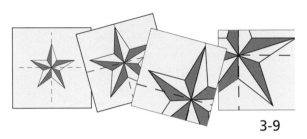

3-9

❸ Piece together the center lines of the enlargements (Figure 3-10).

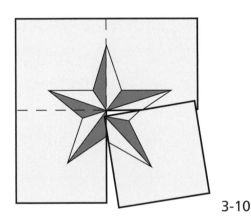

3-10

GRAPH PAPER METHOD

❶ Trace the original design on small block graph paper such as 1/2" (Figure 3-11).

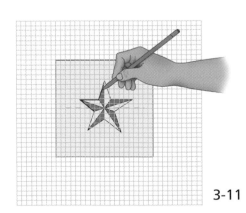

3-11

❷ To enlarge the pattern twice its size, copy the design, block for block, on 1" grid graph paper or for three times its size, copy on 3" grid paper (Figure 3-12).

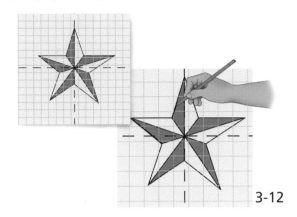

3-12

TRANSFERRING THE DESIGN TO THE CANVAS

CARBON OR GRAPHITE/ TRANSFER PAPER

❶ Tape a sheet of carbon or graphite paper right side down on the canvas (Figure 3-13).

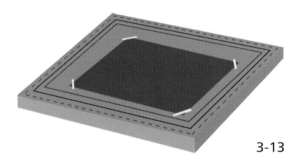

3-13

❷ Tape the design right side up on top of the paper (Figure 3-14). Trace the design with a pencil or ballpoint pen. Apply even pressure to ensure that the design transfers completely to the canvas below. Remove the paper and check for adequate transfer.

3-14

GRAPHITE SHADING

❶ Shade the back side of your design with a soft graphite pencil (such as a #2). If it is a large open design you can simply shade over the lines of the design. However, if the design is more detailed and complex it will be necessary to shade the entire design to ensure that it transfers adequately (Figure 3-15).

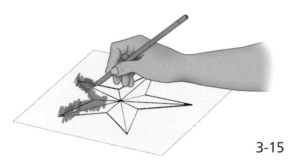

3-15

❷ Place the drawing right side up and secure it on the canvas. Trace the design, applying steady pressure to ensure adequate transfer.

OVERHEAD PROJECTOR

This transfer method works well with open or uncomplicated designs by using clear transparencies to project the image onto the canvas. The image size can be changed by varying the distance between the projector and the canvas. Don't try this with intricate or detailed designs. For these, use an opaque projector.

❶ Trace the design on a clear transparency or piece of acetate with a wax pencil or ink pen.

❷ Stand the stretched canvas against a wall or prop it vertically on a tabletop.

❸ Place the transparency on the projector bed and trace the design on the canvas.

OPAQUE PROJECTOR

This method allows you to alter and project simple or complex designs using opaque images such as photos, drawings, or pictures.

❶ Prop the stretched canvas against a wall or on a tabletop and place the design you want to transfer in the projector.

❷ With a pencil, trace the projected design on the canvas as shown in Figure 3-16.

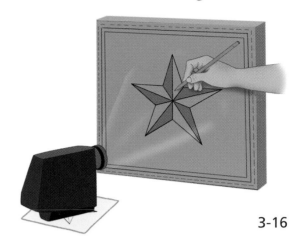

3-16

SEALING YOUR FLOORCLOTH

Applying several coats of protective sealer, whether it be varnish, polyurethane, or wax, is a very important step in the process of making a floorcloth. When done correctly, the floorcloth will wear well and give you many years of enjoyment.

I prefer to use water-based non-yellowing products. Most oil-based products yellow even when the label says they don't. A dull or matte finish provides adequate protection without a sheen. If you prefer a slight sheen, use a matte finish with a top coat of satin. For a highly polished effect (such as marble or stone looks), apply several coats of satin finish.

MATERIALS

~ *Water-based acrylic sealer, varnish, or polyurethane*
~ *4" sponge paint brush, quality bristle brush, or paint pad and paint tray*
~ *Fine grade (220 or 320) sandpaper or steel wool and tack cloth (for fabric appliqué floorcloths only)*

⤳ Carefully stir varnish, never shake it. Shaking causes air bubbles.

⤳ For best results use high quality bristle brushes, sponge brushes, or paint pads. Avoid using paint rollers for varnish—they create bubbles and give the varnish a clouded appearance.

⤳ Tap your brush on the rim of the can instead of wiping it to remove excess sealer. Tapping reduces air bubbles.

⤳ Apply all coats of varnish in the same direction.

Four thin coats of sealer is the minimum requirement for painted floorcloths. If you've applied paper decoupage or fabric appliqué, apply five to six thin coats of sealer to protect and secure the materials glued to the surface.

Always follow the sealer manufacturer's instructions for application and drying time. Apply several thin coats of sealer rather than one thick coat. Allow the canvas to dry completely between each coat. When dry, the canvas should feel room temperature to the touch. If it feels even the least bit cold, the sealer isn't dry. Brush on all the coats in the same direction to minimize brush strokes.

If you miss spots as you're brushing on a coat of sealer, don't brush over them while the varnish is still wet or you'll create visible brush strokes in the varnish. Instead, wait until that coat dries and cover missed spots with the next coat of sealer. Allow the floorcloth to cure for several days before removing it from the stretcher to finish and hem the edges.

❶ Pour the sealer into a shallow dish and let it settle for a few minutes to remove any air bubbles.

❷ Dip the brush into the sealer and tap any excess liquid back into the dish. Drag the brush in long even strokes across the canvas, vertically or horizontally, covering the hem lines (Figure 3-17). Let each coat dry thoroughly.

3-17

❸ Fabric appliqué floorcloths require light sanding with fine sandpaper or steel wool on the top and edges of the fabric motif to remove any rough fibers (Figure 3-18). Do this in a circular motion, being careful not to sand through the fabric. Repeat this light sanding after the first, second, and third coats of sealer have dried, until the fabric is sealed and no longer rough. Carefully wipe the sanding residue away with a tack cloth before applying the next coat of sealer.

3-18

HEMMING THE EDGES

To hem or not to hem? This question comes up in all of my classes. Is hemming really necessary? It's often a question of preference. Many floorcloth artists don't hem their canvases and feel they wear just fine. If the floorcloth will fit an exact space, wall-to-wall, leave the edges raw and install shoe molding on top. In this case, the only area that might need a hem would be in the doorway.

Other artists feel that hemmed floorcloths wear better. I have found that when the edges are turned under, the floorcloth lays completely flat on the floor without curling or fraying edges. This is not only safer, but prevents undue wear and tear.

I've experimented with a variety of hemming methods and have been most satisfied with rubber cement or hot glue. Both types of glue are easy to use and are dry and permanent almost immediately.

The adhesive you choose will depend on the type of canvas, your capabilities, and sensitivity. Rubber cement yields a smooth flat finish but has a strong odor and is suitable for most canvases except "floorcloth" canvas (the glue won't stick to the universal primer on the back of this type of canvas. For this, use hot glue).

Hot glue has no odor but requires some skill and care when handling the glue gun and you must work quickly before the glue dries.

When using any glue, work at room temperature. If the air is cold, the sealer will crack when the hem allowance is folded to the back (a hair dryer works well for warming the area if necessary).

MATERIALS

- ❧ *Rubber cement or high-temp hot glue gun and several high-temp glue sticks*
- ❧ *Craft stick or spatula for burnishing the hem*
- ❧ *Scissors*
- ❧ *Ruler*
- ❧ *Pencil*

SECRETS FOR SUCCESS

❧ *Handle the hot glue gun with care. It can burn you if mishandled.*
❧ *Before starting to hem, check to see if the cut line and fold line are still visible on the right side of the canvas. If not, redraw them.*
❧ *Always miter the corners on the front of the canvas.*

RUBBER CEMENT

❶ Redraw the cut line if it has become obscured by paint or embellishments. Use scissors to cut the canvas off the stretcher at the cut line.

❷ Place the canvas right side up and draw a diagonal line (miter) at each corner across point "A" where the fold lines intersect (Figure 3-19). Cut across this line with a pair of scissors to remove the corner (Figure 3-19 detail). This cut enables you to hem the corners without bulk.

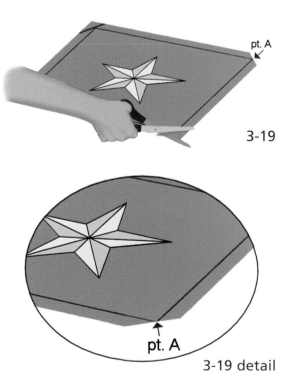

3-19

pt. A

3-19 detail

❸ Measure the hem allowance on the front of the canvas. On the back side of the canvas, draw a gluing guideline double what the hem measures. For example, if the hem allowance is 1", draw the gluing guideline 2" in from the cut edge (Figure 3-20). This shows you where and how far into the canvas to apply the rubber cement.

3-20

❹ Apply a layer of rubber cement from the guideline to the canvas edge around all four sides (Figure 3-20). Let dry until the glue is tacky but not wet. Apply a second coat of rubber cement to ensure proper coverage.

❺ Let the second coat of rubber cement dry until tacky. Begin in the middle of one side and fold and press the hem over the cement, following the fold line on the front of the canvas (Figure 3-21). Burnish with a craft stick or putty knife. Continue folding and burnishing the hem into the corners, creating a smooth flat finish until all four sides are completed (Figure 3-22).

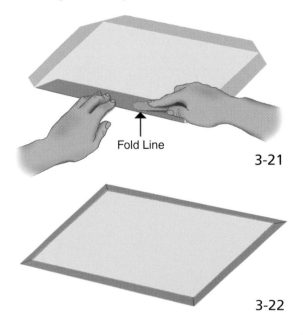

Fold Line

3-21

3-22

GLUE GUN

❶ Follow Steps 1 and 2 in the rubber cement technique.

❷ Start in the middle of one side and follow the fold line to carefully fold the hem allowance to the back side (Figure 3-23). Repeat this for all four sides. This fold gives you a guideline for applying the hot glue.

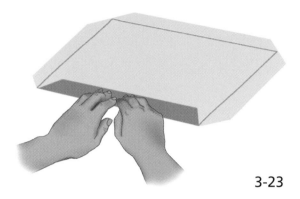

3-23

❸ Turn the canvas to the back and start in the middle of one side. Apply a thin 3" line of hot glue along the hem allowance (Figure 3-24). Be sure to keep the glue on the hem allowance or it will seep out when you turn up the edge. Quickly fold the hem over and carefully burnish it down with a craft stick. The glue is hot, so be careful not to burn yourself. Burnishing will disperse and smooth the glue (Figure 3-25).

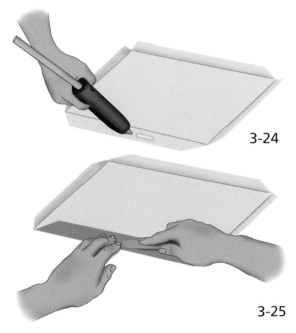

3-24

3-25

❹ Pull the edge of the hem allowance back slightly and apply glue inside the fold and burnish (Figure 3-26). Repeat the gluing process on the other three sides of the canvas. Be sure to apply glue well into the corners and burnish them adequately to prevent any lumps.

3-26

HEMMING CIRCULAR FLOORCLOTHS

Hemming circular floorcloths is easier than you think. I've found that rubber cement works best because of the way the edges are handled. Small cuts from the outer edge to the marked fold line help the canvas fold evenly around the curve. The distance between the cuts varies, depending on the degree of the curve—the smaller the floorcloth, the closer together the cuts should be and vice versa. Determine the correct spacing of the cuts by experimenting on a scrap piece of canvas or paper.

❶ Cut the canvas from the frame along the cut line.

❷ On a scrap piece of canvas, experiment with cuts along the curve to determine how far apart they should be for the hem to curve correctly along the fold line.

❸ Lay the canvas right side up on the work surface and use a pencil to mark dots at even intervals along the fold line.

❹ Use sharp scissors to make small cuts from the outer edge to the dot on the fold line (Figure 3-27).

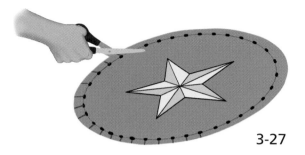

3-27

Cut precisely to the fold line—cuts that end before the fold line will create points along the curve when the canvas is turned under and cuts that go beyond the fold line into the design will create dips in the curve.

❺ Measure the hem allowance on the front of the canvas. On the back side of the canvas, draw a gluing guideline double what the hem measures. For example, if the hem allowance is 1", draw the gluing guideline 2" in from the cut edge. This shows you where and how far into the canvas to apply the rubber cement (Figure 3-28). Apply two coats of rubber cement, allowing each one to dry until tacky.

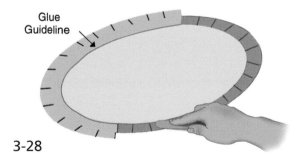

Glue Guideline

3-28

❻ Fold the clipped edges to the backside and burnish with a craft stick (Figure 3-28). Each flap or clipped edge will overlap the flap proceeding it. Although this method does create some bulk in the hem, the bulk is even and consistent and therefore any wear will be gradual and even as well.

CARING FOR YOUR FLOORCLOTH

Because the damage from shoes and furniture legs is maximized when your canvas is placed on carpet or padded surfaces, I recommend placing your floorcloth on hard floors such as wood, vinyl, tile, cement, or marble. Try to avoid using floorcloths in areas that are very wet unless the canvas has been double primed and sealed on both sides. Always use chair leg protectors to prevent scratches in the floorcloth's varnish.

You can use mild dish soap and warm water to clean any dirt from the canvas, but don't use scouring products because they will scratch and eventually erode the sealer.

Over time, small fissure cracks or "crazing" may appear in the sealer. This is an inherent quality and is virtually unnoticeable if the cloth is kept clean.

If you find the sealer is wearing thin, you may need to reseal the floorcloth. If the surface is shiny, sand it lightly to remove the sheen. It's best to stretch the cloth again to prevent buckling and puckering. Simply tack it to a stretcher or flat frame with thumb tacks or small nails or brads along the outside edge through the fold line (Figure 3-29). Apply several coats of sealer

and let it cure for several days before putting it back on the floor.

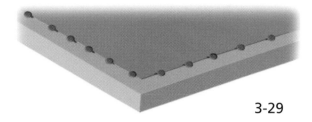

3-29

Never fold a floorcloth! Folding cracks the sealer and creates permanent creases in the canvas. Instead, roll it into a tube shape with the design side out (Figure 3-30) and place it in or around a tube. Wrap it in paper, not plastic, for protection. If the floorcloth is decorated with paper or fabric, it will be somewhat stiff because of the embellishments glued to its surface, so roll it loosely.

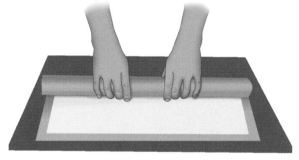

3-30

CHAPTER 4:
DECORATING YOUR FLOORCLOTH

PAINTED APPLICATIONS

Decorating your floorcloth is a very exciting step—when the piece really comes to life. There are so many ways to apply paint that choosing one can be a bit daunting. Each method produces a beautiful effect and when the methods are combined or added to other embellishing techniques, the final outcome can be remarkable.

The techniques in this chapter range from easy to moderately difficult, based on the amount of skill, time, and effort needed to master each. Choose from "freehand techniques" such as fringe, lattice, crescents, and veining or try "assisted applications" such as taping, checkerboards, doily spraying, and stamping. Be patient and practice, practice, practice. Try your hand at several techniques and create your own unique piece of art.

FREEHAND PAINTING

Look around your home for designs to use on your floorcloth. Fabric, wallpaper, wrapping paper, or magazines provide a variety of ideas and designs. The charm of "handmade" is evident in freehand work, where lines, colors, or patterns vary in size, shape, or overall proportion (as shown in the plaid floorcloth). Patterns can be hard-edged and geometric or free and flowing.

Freehand designs can be produced with acrylic paints, paint pens, markers, or colored pencils, to name just a few.

LATTICE

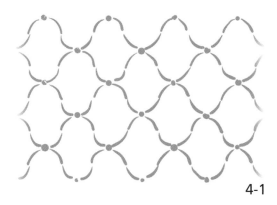

4-1

Lattice is not only simple to create, but sophisticated in style. Because it's more an accent motif than an independent design, I usually combine it with one or two other embellishing techniques such as a paper decoupage border and painted fringe. Lattice can be stenciled, hand-painted, or freehand drawn, depending on your artistic ability and preference. The instructions below are a freehand application with paint pens or markers.

MATERIALS
∾ *Paint pen or marker*
∾ *Pencil*
∾ *Ruler*
∾ *Gum or plastic artist's eraser*

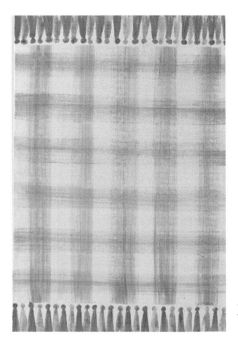

A freehand plaid pattern is easy. The drybrush method creates the illusion of woven cloth.

① Divide the canvas length and width into equal parts. With a light pencil, connect the marks with diagonal lines, forming the latticework (Figure 4-2).

4-2

② With a paint pen or marker, make dots where the lines intersect. Draw in curved crescent shapes as shown (Figure 4-3). Erase your original pencil lines when the lattice is complete and dry.

4-3

CRESCENTS

4-4

Painted crescents are a quick and easy way to embellish a floorcloth when you want a fresh contemporary look. This is a simple freehand technique done by dry-brushing. Use bristle brushes in several sizes to create the streaked/washed effect. Because the pattern creates a sense of movement, only simple borders are needed to finish the design.

MATERIALS
∾ *Acrylic paints of choice*
∾ *1" and 2" flat bristle brushes*
∾ *Palette*
∾ *Paper towels*
∾ *Water*

① Pencil in the placement of each large crescent shape for painting reference. Dip a 2" bristle brush into one paint color and wipe off most of the color on a paper towel. This will help to create the streaked effect.

4-5

Apply the paint in a sweeping curved motion. You may need to go over the area several times to produce the desired streaked effect (Figure 4-5). Let dry. Finish one color before starting a new one and let dry.

❷ Apply the smaller crescent shapes with a 1" bristle brush, allowing some to overlap the larger shapes already painted (Figure 4-6).

4-6

PUZZLE PAINTING

4-7

Puzzle painting is used for accent work or detailing. This technique coordinates and often highlights the main design, but is rarely seen alone. It resembles interlocking puzzle pieces and is created by drawing many intertwined curved lines in a confined area with a variety of paint pens, markers, or colored pencils. The technique is fun and makes an impressive border for a variety of floorcloth designs.

Decorative puzzle painting lends color, pattern, and texture to this otherwise ordinary stained glass design.

MATERIALS
❧ *Paint pens, markers, or colored pencils*

❶ With a paint pen or marker, draw squiggle lines that curve in and around each other. The lines can stop and start as many times as needed to create the effect (Figure 4-8).

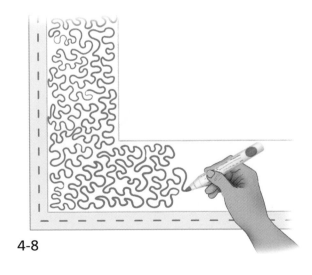

4-8

SWIRLS, CURLS & WAVES

4-9

Whimsical designs such as these are not only fun to draw, but quick to finish. The simple patterns can be incorporated into a variety of decorating styles by simply changing the color scheme—primary colors for a child's room, subtle shades for a contemporary living room, or neutral tones for a classical bedroom. The designs can be done with paint pens, markers, colored pencils, or thinned acrylic paint in squeeze bottles and are meant to vary a bit in size and shape, so relax and have fun!

MATERIALS

- *Paint pens, markers, or acrylic paints*
- *Pencil or fading marking pen*
- *Squeeze bottles and water (if using paints)*

❶ *Swirls*: Pencil in the size swirl desired. Place the point of the pen at the center of the swirl and move the pen clockwise or counter-clockwise around the center until it's complete (Figure 4-10).

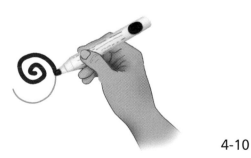

4-10

❷ *Curls:* This design consists of three parts: two swirls and a curved line in between. Follow the instructions for making the swirl then add a curved line and another swirl at the opposite end. Create another curl intersecting the first (Figure 4-11).

4-11

❸ *Waves:* Pencil in guidelines for the placement of the waves then paint over the marks in one continuous motion (Figure 4-12). Add accent dots in coordinating or complementary colors.

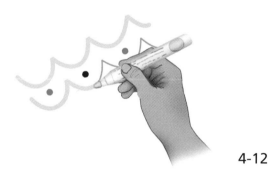

4-12

BORDERS

Borders are an important design element that create visual boundaries around the edges of objects.

Borders can be plain or fancy, geometric or curvy, solid or multicolored. No matter the design, the purpose is the same—to enclose a space, in this case the central design, and to keep your eye inside the border enjoying the artwork.

The border you choose depends on your artistic ability and the amount of time you want to spend. Intricate borders are well worth the work, but take quite a bit of time, while solid borders are simple and quick. It's a good idea to make a variety of borders on poster board and lay them next to the central design to help you decide which type to use.

SOLID BORDERS

4-13

There are two ways to add a solid border: freehand painting or taping. Borders painted freehand are the most simple to paint, requiring only acrylic paint and a paint brush. However, you need a fairly steady hand to make the straight lines and I recommend practicing first.

"Harlequin," courtesy of Martha Miller. The borders and diamonds in this floorcloth were created with a simple taping method.

Taping is the most widely used method for painting solid borders. It's a bit more work but produces fabulous results. Simply tape off the outside edges of the area you want to paint. To create clean crisp lines, burnish the taped edges well with a craft stick or plastic putty knife to prevent paint from bleeding underneath and use as dry a brush as possible with undiluted paint.

MATERIALS
✺ *Painter's masking tape*
✺ *Acrylic paint*
✺ *Sponge paint brush approximately the width of the border*
✺ *Craft knife*
✺ *Pencil*
✺ *Craft stick or plastic putty knife for burnishing*
✺ *Ruler, triangle, or "L" ruler*
✺ *Palette*

❶ Using a ruler, mark the length and width of the border around the perimeter of the canvas. Apply painter's masking tape along the outside of the border, trimming the inside corners "A" and "B" with a craft knife. Burnish the inside taped edges of the border to prevent any paint from seeping under the tape (Figure 4-14). Burnish several times to ensure adequate sealing.

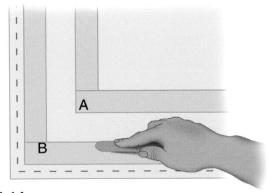

4-14

❷ Apply a thin coat of acrylic paint, starting on the tape and dragging the brush into the border (Figure 4-15). Let dry and apply a second coat of color. Remove the tape when the paint is tacky, not dry, to prevent the paint from peeling.

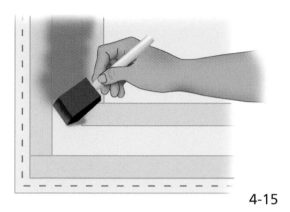

4-15

CHECKERED BORDERS

4-16

Checkered borders add an element of fun to decorative designs. They can be applied by outlining, taping, stenciling, or stamping. The method illustrated is a simple outlining technique that eliminates the task of taping off each box and creates a dazzling border in a short time.

MATERIALS
∽ *Black paint pen or marker*
∽ *Acrylic paints to match*
∽ *Flat artist's brush*
∽ *Ruler*
∽ *Pencil*

❶ Draw in the length and width of the desired border on the canvas. Add a square in each corner (Figure 4-17).

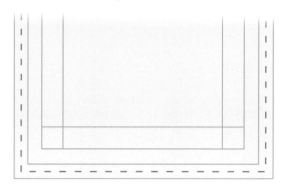

4-17

❷ Measure the length and width of the border, inside the corner squares, and divide it into equal parts. For example, if the inside border measures 3" wide x 18" long, the border can have one row of nine rectangles 3" wide x 2" long or two rows of nine rectangles that are 1½" wide x 2" long (Figure 4-18).

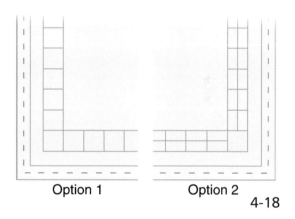

Option 1   Option 2

4-18

❸ Use a ruler as a guide and outline each box you'll be painting black with a black paint pen or marker (Figure 4-19). You can paint the corner squares black or an accent color from the center design. Fill in each box, using a flat artist's brush and matching acrylic paint or the paint pen. Let dry and apply another coat if necessary.

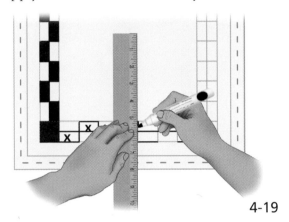

4-19

FREEHAND FRINGE & ROPING

4-20

Fringe and roping are two types of decorator trims used to adorn the edges of home decorating items such as pillows, draperies, and area rugs. Painted fringe and roping are unique ways to add the finishing touch to your floorcloth.

Before trying fringing and roping on your floorcloth, practice on poster board, using samples of the real thing for reference. You may choose to paint on just fringe, just roping, or both, multicolored or solid, depending on the floorcloth design.

Painted fringe is a moderately difficult technique created by painting sets of knots and bell-shaped fringe along the two short sides of the floorcloth. Shading with three colors creates a three-dimensional effect.

A selection of fringe and roping coordinated with wallpaper borders and other decorative trims used to adorn centers, borders, and corners.

A rope border is made with a succession of S-shaped motifs painted side-by-side around the entire outside edge of the floorcloth. Although somewhat time consuming, it's very easy to do.

FRINGE

MATERIALS
❧ Acrylic paints: 1 light, 1 medium, 1 dark
❧ Brushes: medium round artist's brush small round artist's brush
❧ Ruler
❧ Tape
❧ Pencil
❧ Paper plate palette
❧ Water

❶ Determine the size fringe you want and pencil in guidelines indicating the placement and size of the knots and fringe. Sketch four or five knots and the bell shapes for the fringe placement, allowing the bell shapes to overlap each other a bit (Figure 4-21).

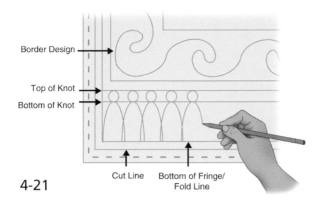

Border Design
Top of Knot
Bottom of Knot
Cut Line   Bottom of Fringe/ Fold Line

4-21

❷ Thin a dab of the darkest color paint on a paper plate with a drop or two of water. Using a medium round artist's brush, fill in the first knot. To paint the fringe, start at the meeting point of the knot and the bell. Pull the brush down to the bottom of the bell, allowing the brush strokes to overlap. This will create a streaked effect to simulate the yarns of actual fringe. Continue painting one knot and one bell shape at a time (Figure 4-22). Let dry.

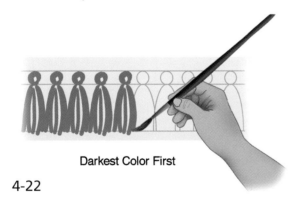

Darkest Color First

4-22

❸ Using a small round brush, apply the medium color to only the center area of each knot and bell shape in the same manner as Step 2 (Figure 4-23). Let dry.

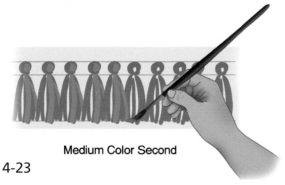

Medium Color Second

4-23

❹ Apply the lightest highlight color, again to the center of each knot and fringe (Figure 4-24). Be careful not to completely cover the first two colors.

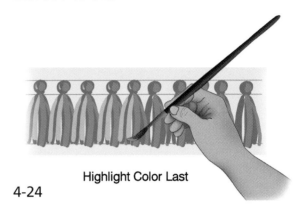

Highlight Color Last

4-24

ROPING

4-25

MATERIALS
∾ Flat artist's brushes in width of desired S-shape (one for each paint color)
∾ Acrylic paints in two (or more) colors
∾ Pencil
∾ Ruler
∾ Water
∾ Palette
∾ Tape

❶ Pencil in the guideline for the rope border around the perimeter of the canvas. Apply and burnish tape along the outside edges of the border to protect the other areas and produce a clean edge.

❷ Beginning approximately 1/4" in from a corner, paint a slanted S-shape with one color, then another with a second color (Figure 4-26). You may want to use more than two colors. Continue painting S-shapes, alternating colors, until you reach the corner.

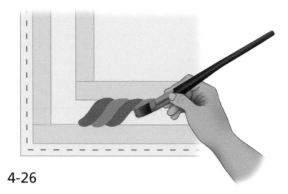

4-26

3 Curve the S-shapes around the corner (Figure 4-27). Continue painting S-shapes until the entire border is completed.

4-27

STENCILS, STAMPS & PATTERNS

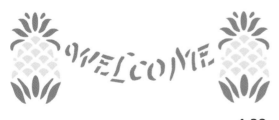

4-28

STENCILING

This decorative effect is done with a stencil made of mylar, plastic, or acetate. Precut stencils can be purchased individually or in packets for multicolored designs. You can also design and cut your own stencils with a craft knife or electric stencil cutter.

Basic stenciling is relatively simple—just secure the stencil to the canvas with tape and use a bristle stencil brush to apply the paint. You can achieve a sense of depth by using several different shades of the same color or hand-painting over particular areas to highlight the design.

Use stencil creme paint, artist's tube acrylics, craft acrylic paints, oil tubes, or oil stencil crayons. Because the creme and crayon paints are dry, not liquid, they provide a smooth finish with clean crisp edges. Liquid acrylic paints create a nice finish too, but you'll spend more time and care removing most of the paint from the brush so it doesn't seep under the stencil edges.

Good quality stencil brushes are essential. Inexpensive brushes shed bristles and lose their shape quickly. If possible, use a separate brush for each color and match the size of the brush to the general size of the cut designs.

The stencil technique shown here is done with a single multicolored stencil and creme stencil paint.

MATERIALS
∾ Precut stencil (purchased or handmade)
∾ Creme stencil paints or acrylic paints
∾ Stencil brushes in several sizes
∾ Tape
∾ Paper plates
∾ Pencil
∾ Paper towels

① Tape the stencil in place and lightly mark the stencil and canvas with a vertical and horizontal center line registration in case you need to remove it and replace it in the same spot (Figure 4-29).

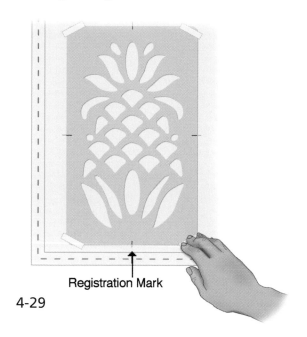

Registration Mark

4-29

Stencil one color at a time and tape over all the areas you're not working on. Here the green leaves are taped over while yellow is being applied to the body of the pineapple (Figure 4-30).

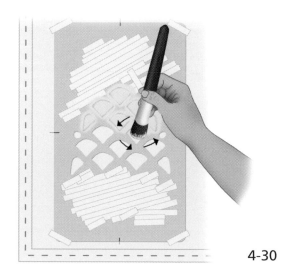

4-30

② Rub the brush in yellow stencil creme or acrylic paint to distribute the paint evenly. Dab off the excess paint on a paper towel.

Move the brush in a circular motion inside the cut areas, being careful not to push paint under the cut edges (Figure 4-30). Let dry.

③ Remove the tape from the green areas and tape over the yellow body of the pineapple. Stencil the green areas, repeating the same process (Figure 4-31). Remove the tape and stencil and let dry. If you have several motifs to paint, you may want to stencil one color throughout and go back to the next color.

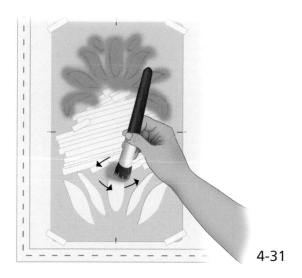

4-31

STAMPING

4-32

Many of today's popular designs are achieved by stamping. Whether the stamps are made of rubber, sponge, precut foam, vegetables, or wood, they give you the ability to create simple or complex designs in a short time. Precut stamps are available in a vast variety of subjects ranging from geometric shapes, brick paths, and flowers, to alphabets, country hearts, and mosaic tiles.

The techniques for brick and foliage stamping are detailed below. You can use these same steps for almost any type of stamped design.

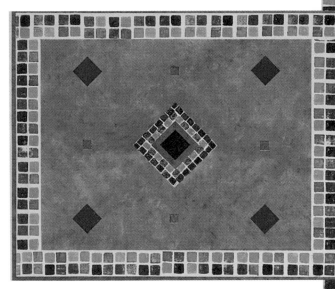

Mosaic tile floorcloths created with balsa wood and foam stamps.

A popular fleur de lis pattern applied with a rubber stamp.

BRICKS

1 Basecoat the canvas with a color that simulates the grout in the brick pattern (ivory, grey, taupe). Let dry. Tape off the outside edge of the brick area. Measure the sponge, then add 1/4" to its length and width to allow space for the background color/grout to show between each row of bricks. Draw the rows of brick on the canvas, using the measurements of the sponge plus 1/4" (Figure 4-33).

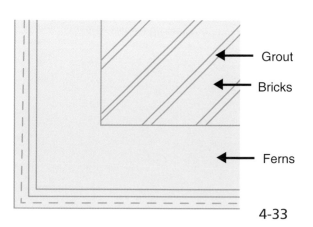

Grout

Bricks

Ferns

4-33

2 Pour a small amount of peach and rust paint in a spiral pattern on a paper plate (Figure 4-34). Pour only rust paint on a second plate. Lightly place the sponge in the first plate of paint once and then again. Dab off the excess paint on a paper towel.

4-34

3 Place the sponge on the canvas inside the drawn guidelines and press firmly. Leave space between each stamp for the background/grout color to show through. Alternate dipping the sponge in the peach/rust paint and rust to vary the color and shades of each brick. Finish an entire line before starting a new one (Figure 4-35). Alternate the placement of bricks in the remaining rows and continue stamping until all the bricks are in place.

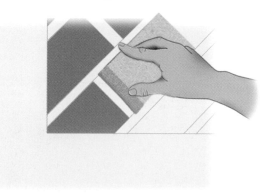

4-35

FERNS

❶ Use a flat artist's brush to apply acrylic paint to the cut side of the stamp. You can create a shaded effect by applying several shades of green at once (Figure 4-36).

4-36

❷ Place the stamp in position and press it firmly on the canvas. Carefully lift the stamp off the canvas and stamp again once or twice without repainting the stamp, turning the stamp in a different direction. This will create a layered and shaded effect. Apply varying shades of green paint to the stamp as needed. Continue stamping the ferns until the entire area has been completed (Figure 4-37).

4-37

DOILY SPRAY

4-38

Paper and fabric doilies have been a favorite decoration for food, tabletops and furniture for more than a century. The intricate patterns are so popular that artists have found a number of ways to simulate their elaborate designs on just about any surface. My favorite technique is doily spray because it's relatively easy and the results are spectacular. Simply secure a paper doily to the canvas and spray over it with acrylic paint. When you remove the doily, the lovely intricate pattern is revealed.

Doily spray looks lovely alone or combined with other techniques like a sponged background and a rope border or a color-washed background and a fringe border. Using the doilies for decoupage is not recommended because the paper will pucker when wet.

MATERIALS

- *Paper doilies (I used "Basket Lace Square" courtesy of Royal Lace)*
- *Paint:*
  base coat—ivory exterior latex house paint
  background—blue acrylic spray paint
  accent—rose acrylic craft paint
- *Brushes:*
  4" sponge brush
  small round artist's brush
- *Repositionable spray adhesive*
- *Paint palette/paper plates*
- *Pencil*
- *Ruler*
- *Craft stick or plastic putty knife for burnishing*

❶ Using a 4" sponge brush or roller, basecoat the canvas with two coats of ivory (this will be the color of the doily when it's finished). Let dry between coats. Trim the doilies as desired, position them on the canvas, and lightly trace the outline of each to use as a gluing guideline (Figure 4-39).

4-39

❷ Remove the doilies from the canvas and spray the fronts with two coats of repositionable spray adhesive. Follow the manufacturer's instructions for proper application and let dry between coats. Place each doily in position on the canvas and burnish well with a craft stick or plastic putty knife.

❸ Lay the canvas flat on the floor and carefully spray the entire canvas with blue spray paint, covering all the ivory background (Figure 4-40). You can only spray the canvas once, so be sure the ivory background is completely covered. Apply an even coat to prevent drips.

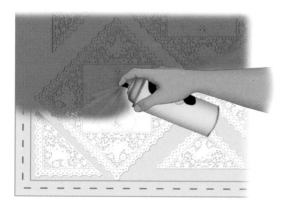

4-40

The doilies will begin to shrivel and pucker as they absorb the paint. To prevent the paper from sticking to the paint, carefully peel off the doilies before the paint sets up. Let the paint dry thoroughly.

❹ Using a small round artist's brush, fill in the center and border dots with rose paint, following the dotted pattern on the doily. (Figure 4-41).

4-41

FAUX FINISHES

This green and white fantasy marble is created with water-based paints and glazes.

Transform your floorcloth into a dazzling work of art with a faux finish—a fabulous way to customize your floorcloth and add richness and texture to the design and overall appearance. Sponging, color washing, and veining are just a few of the many water-based finishes you can use. Other trompe l'oeil (fool the eye) effects, such as faux animal skins, are worth trying too.

"Cheetah," courtesy of Amy Donavan.

This method of sponging is done with latex or craft acrylic paint straight from the container. Color washing and veining are done with colored glazes which produce transparent, three-dimensional effects.

A glaze is a paint or pigment mixed with a glazing medium and thinned to the point of translucency. A glazing medium adds body and transparency to a paint. Either Floetrol (a latex paint conditioner), water-based varnish, or water-based glazing liquid can be used as a glazing medium for colored glazes. The recipe shown here uses Floetrol as the glazing medium.

Premixed water-based colored glazes work equally well and are available in paint, craft, and art supply stores.

Practice is essential to produce realistic finishes, so gather some poster board and the list of materials and see what you can do!

Sponge Painting

4-42

Sponging is one of several finishes that create the illusion of texture. Different sponges produce different textures—depending mostly on the shape of the sponge and the size of its pores. A smooth small-pored sponge will create a fairly

Create subtle texture with exhilarating colors using a simple one-color sponging technique.

smooth fine texture and a rough large-pored sponge will produce a more coarse and bumpy appearance. Natural sea, kitchen, ceramic, and cosmetic sponges all yield interesting and unique effects. Experiment with several sponges before you choose one for your design.

Sponging is easiest with water-soluble paints such as premixed latex paint or small bottles of acrylic craft paint.

When the paint colors are applied directly on the canvas with a sponge, it's known as *sponging-on. Sponging-off* is when one color of paint is rolled on and then removed in some areas with a sponge. Because it takes more time to sponge paint off the canvas, oil-based paints (which are slow-drying) work best for sponging-off.

Depending on the color scheme, the colors can be applied together or separately over a chosen background color. When two colors are applied together, three colors will show on the canvas (two sponging colors and the color they make when mixed). If you want each color to show individually, apply each separately and allow it to dry before applying the next.

This technique can be applied over a background color or directly over the primed canvas.

MATERIALS

- ❧ *Sponge*
- ❧ *Acrylic paint in several colors*
- ❧ *Paper plates*
- ❧ *Paper towels*
- ❧ *Optional: Exterior latex background paint*

---

❶ Basecoat the canvas with two coats of background color and let dry. Dampen the sponge and wring out any excess water. Pour paint into several squeeze bottles and swirl each color onto one paper plate (Figure 4-43). Dip the sponge directly in the plate of paint. Don't push the sponge around the plate or the colors will mix and become muddy. Lift the sponge out and repeat several times.

4-43

❷ Randomly sponge paint on the canvas using a staccato up-and-down motion and changing the position of your wrist and the sponge (Figure 4-44). Fill in as much or as little of the background as you choose to achieve the effect you want.

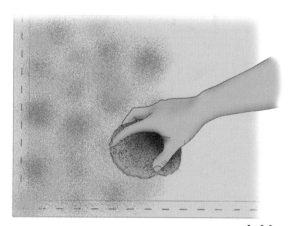

4-44

Color Washing

4-45

Color washing can create many different subtle effects such as parchment, sandstone, adobe plaster, and distressed textures.

Color washing is easiest when mixed into a colored glaze of water-based paint, Floetrol (a paint conditioner) or another type of glazing liquid, and water. Water-based paints are easy to clean up and fast drying, so you'll accomplish the job in a relatively short period of time.

The glaze recipe below will produce a translucent finish. Wipe or brush this glaze mixture on the canvas in a random pattern to create an uneven effect. The key to producing an attractive finish is to apply the glaze in different thicknesses—some areas thin, others a bit heavier, blending with a dry brush or rag as you go. For a more subtle effect, apply two coats of wash, allowing the first coat to dry for 24 hours before applying the second coat.

MATERIALS

- ❧ Exterior latex paint for background
- ❧ Acrylic or latex paint for glaze color
- ❧ 2 bristle brushes
- ❧ Paper plates
- ❧ Floetrol (latex paint conditioner) or other type of glazing liquid
- ❧ Water
- ❧ Mixing container/measuring cup

GLAZE RECIPE

1 part acrylic or latex paint
1 part Floetrol (glazing liquid)
2 parts water

❶ Basecoat the canvas using a sponge brush or roller. Let dry. In a mixing container, mix the color wash glaze. Dip the bristle brush in the glaze, wiping off the excess. Randomly apply the glaze in a criss-cross fashion using a dry brush to catch any dripping glaze and to soften the connecting edges. Some areas will naturally be heavier and more opaque, while other areas will be lighter with more background showing through (Figure 4-46). This technique can also be accomplished using a large sponge. Simply dip the sponge in the colored glaze and wipe it across the canvas in the same random pattern. This produces a softer, more muted texture than the brush.

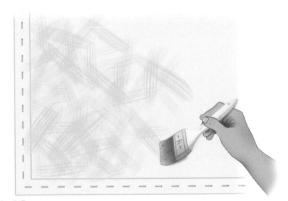

4-46

Veining

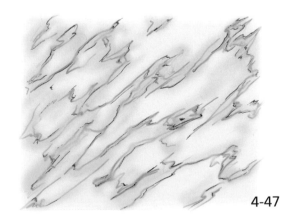

4-47

Veining is a simple way to achieve a faux marbled effect. The background could be a combination of sponging or ragging, but it won't look like a piece of marble until the veins are applied. If you have a specific marbling effect in mind, study a sample or photo of the real thing to determine the thickness, length, pattern, and coloration of the veining. If you want to create an abstract marbling or fantasy finish, you can be more freeform.

You can create veining with assorted sizes of paint brushes, erasers, and feathers. Paint veins with one or two colors, then add a third darker or contrasting color for definition and highlighting.

To create a realistic effect, make a glaze from the recipe below. Applying several thin translucent coats will simulate the many layers of stone and add a sense of depth. When using a feather, hold it like you would a knife, not a pencil. The veins are created with the top half of the feather—the tip, edge, and both flat sides. The key to realistic looking veins is to shake and turn your hand as you are painting—producing a crooked line that varies in thickness and density.

GLAZE RECIPE

1 part acrylic paint
1 part Floetrol (glazing liquid)
1 part water

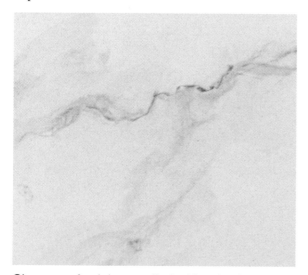

Close up of veining applied with a feather.

1 Basecoat the canvas with two coats of white exterior house paint. Let dry between coats. Lightly pencil the large veining pattern (also known as a drift pattern) on the canvas as a painting guideline. The veins should run in a somewhat diagonal direction, simulating real marble (Figure 4-48).

4-48

2 Follow the glaze recipe for each of the shades of grey, mixing each in a separate cup. For the black glaze, add two parts water to the glaze to achieve a more transparent look. Dip a bristle or sponge brush in the lightest colored grey glaze and paint over the pencil lines, following the pattern and shaking the brush to create an erratic effect (Figure 4-49). Because the paint dries quickly, do one section at a time.

4-49

❸ Use a rag to randomly dab off areas of the glaze to create soft, mottled areas (Figure 4-50).

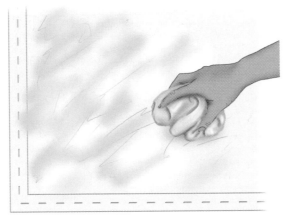

4-50

❹ Dip the feather into the medium grey glaze and accent the top or bottom areas of the large veining patterns to achieve some variation and depth (Figure 4-51). Before the glaze sets up, drag the soft bristle brush over the medium-colored glaze perpendicular to the direction it was applied (Figure 4-52). This will pull the paint away from the vein and give it a more realistic look. Let dry. Again, do only one section at a time.

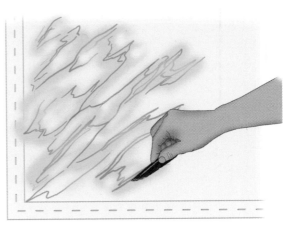

4-51

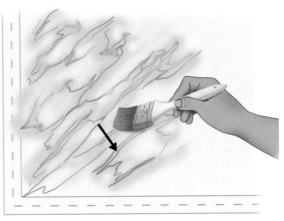

4-52

❺ Dip the feather into the black glaze and accent random areas of the original vein, thus creating a layered effect (Figure 4-53). Soften parts of the vein lines with the soft bristle brush.

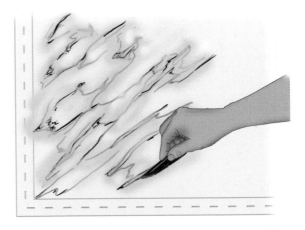

4-53

CHAPTER 5:
OTHER
EMBELLISHMENTS

PAPER DECOUPAGE

(Above) Supplies used in the designing and making of the Classical Table Runner using paper decoupage.

Paper decoupage is a vintage art where decorative paper is glued to the surface of objects and sealed with several coats of clear varnish. This is an innovative and easy way to recycle leftover papers and transform a floorcloth into an inspiring work of art. The best thing about it is that you can quickly create detailed designs with a minimum of artistic ability.

A floorcloth with paper decoupage is more fragile than an all-painted one, so it's best to place it in dry, less traveled areas or under a piece of furniture where it will be protected from everyday wear and tear. If you do put it in a main hallway or heavy traffic area, periodically check the surface for varnish erosion. You may need to reseal the floorcloth occasionally to protect the paper motifs from wearing away.

Papers that work well for decoupage are gift wrap paper, wrapping tissue paper, paper napkins, wallpaper, and color or black and white photocopies. Heavier papers such as note cards and calendar paper are often too bulky and will wear unevenly.

Because paper absorbs moisture and curls

(Above) A selection of papers suitable for decorative application. Clockwise from top: wrapping paper, paper napkin, wallpaper border, color copy, and wrapping tissue paper.

after glue is applied, it's best to work with pieces approximately eight inches or smaller. Unless you're piecing a border or using thin papers (tissue or paper napkins), avoid overlapping pieces of paper. Instead, glue the motifs next to each other to reduce bulk and the amount of sealer needed.

Plan the design so that at least 25% of the canvas is clear of paper. When you add paper to the canvas, it becomes stiff and will be difficult to roll up for storage. A canvas completely covered with paper would be impossible to roll up and wouldn't wear as well.

You can apply paper cutouts for designs or make borders from strips of copy paper or wallpaper. If using black and white copies, it's easiest to paint the copies before you glue them to the canvas. To eliminate the painstaking task of cutting out the small detailed areas in the motif, paint the canvas with a background color that matches the background color of the paper designs. If you have access to a color photocopy machine, you only need to paint one black and white copy and make as many color copies as you need.

DECOUPAGE CUTOUTS

Black and white photocopies are used as the primary decorative medium in this paper decoupage table runner.

Create this unusual, but simple harlequin design with gift wrap paper and metallic paint.

MATERIALS

- ∾ *Wallpaper, photocopies (color or black & white), or gift wrap paper*
- ∾ *Paint:*
  background—exterior latex house paint
  designs—ivory acrylic paint
- ∾ *Brushes:*
  4" sponge paint brush or roller small round artist's brush
- ∾ *Mod Podge or wallpaper adhesive*
- ∾ *Plastic putty knife or craft stick for burnishing*
- ∾ *Sharp scissors or craft knife*
- ∾ *Paper towels*

❶ With a sponge brush or roller, apply two coats of basecoat color to the canvas. Allow to dry between coats.

❷ Make black and white photocopies of the design (in this case a Greek figure). Using a small artist's brush, apply a wash (1 part ivory acrylic paint, 1 part water) over each motif and let dry. This will soften the lines and create a somewhat aged appearance.

❸ Trim the background from around the outside edge of the design using sharp scissors or a craft knife. Paint the intricate background areas of the paper motifs with the latex background paint to match the background color of the canvas (Figure 5-1).

5-1

❹ Working with one motif at a time, apply an even coat of adhesive to the back of the paper cutout (Figure 5-2a) and to the canvas where the cutout is to be placed (Figure 5-2b).

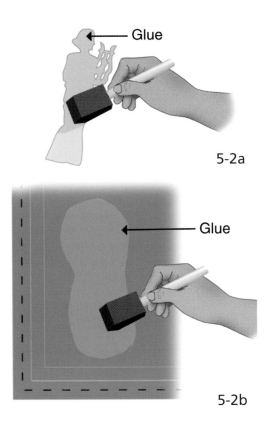

Glue

5-2a

Glue

5-2b

❺ Position the cutout design on the canvas and use a plastic putty knife to smooth the paper from the center to the outside edges to expel excess glue and air bubbles (Figure 5-3). Wipe away any remaining glue with a paper towel.

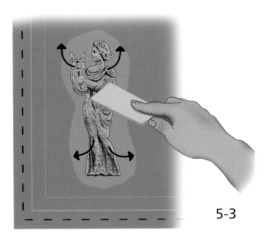

5-3

DECOUPAGE BORDERS

This wallpaper is from Imperial Wallcoverings, Inc., pattern #JH8053B.

It's easy to create a border with strips of paper glued around the edge of the floor-cloth. Try to match the pattern when adding the next strip (similar to matching wallpaper). Most paper borders (with the exception of wallpaper) should be pieced in lengths no longer than 8". Wallpaper can be cut in one piece the length of each side, but should be glued to the canvas in 6"-8" sections, unrolling it backwards as you go. Always add an extra inch of paper to the finished length to accommodate overlapping the corners and for trimming.

When making a border with photo-copies, calculate the number of copies of the design you'll need by dividing the total of the floorcloth border area by the length of the design repeat or piece of paper, adding 1" per piece for overlapping. Make additional copies for matching patterns or mistakes.

Corners can be mitered or straight pieced. When mitering, glue one end piece over the corner and trim. Glue the second end piece over the first and cut on the diagonal. For straight piecing, cut the ends off straight, overlapping the second piece over the first. Either option works for wallpaper borders, although mitering is preferable for patterns with stripes.

You can choose a background color to match the background color of the paper or pull out an accent color to enhance the paper's design.

⚘ *Wallpaper, photocopies (color or black & white), or gift wrap paper*
⚘ *Paint:*
   background—exterior latex house paint to match or complement the paper border designs—acrylics of choice
⚘ *Brushes:*
   2" sponge paint brush
   4" sponge paint brush
⚘ *Mod Podge or wallpaper adhesive*
⚘ *Plastic putty knife or craft stick*
⚘ *Sharp scissors/craft knife*
⚘ *Paper towels*

❶ Paint the background with two coats of exterior latex paint. Let dry between coats. Draw the cut line, fold line, and inside and outside border lines on the canvas as placement guides (Figure 5-4).

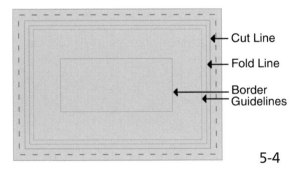

Cut Line
Fold Line
Border Guidelines

5-4

❷ If using wallpaper, cut four strips the length of each side, plus 1" for overlapping the corners. If using wrapping or copy paper, calculate the number of strips you'll need to make a complete border, using approximately 6"-8" pieces of paper. Add 1" to the length of each strip for overlapping and matching. Determine the placement of each strip on the canvas, matching the pattern as needed. Number the back of each strip consecutively to prevent a mix-up during the gluing process.

❸ If using wallpaper, apply glue with the 2" sponge brush to the first 6"-8" of the back of strip #1 and to the corresponding area on the canvas. If using wrapping or copy paper, apply glue to the back of strip #1 (which should be no longer than 8") and to the corresponding area on the canvas (Figure 5-5a and 5-5b).

Glue   5-5a

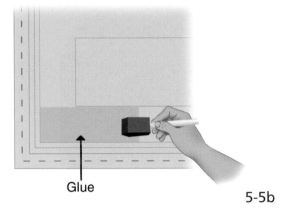

Glue   5-5b

❹ Place the wallpaper or border strip along the guideline over the glue, overlapping the drawn corner about 1/2". Use a putty knife to smooth the paper, moving from the center to the outside edges to remove excess glue and air bubbles (Figure 5-6). Wipe away any excess glue.

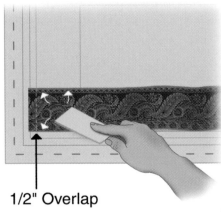

1/2" Overlap

5-6

5 Align a straight edge with the guideline and trim the excess paper from the corner with a craft knife (Figure 5-7). Burnish the paper again.

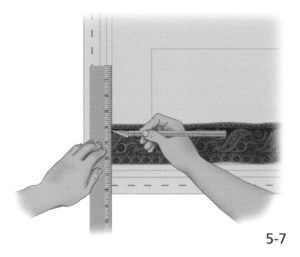

5-7

6 If using wallpaper, glue the remainder of piece #1 in 6"-8" sections along the guideline to the next corner. Burnish and trim the second corner in the same manner as the first. If using wrapping or copy paper, glue one strip at a time, working clockwise around the edge of the canvas. Overlap each preceding strip by about 1/2" (Figure 5-8).

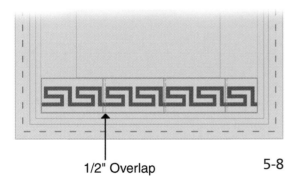

1/2" Overlap   5-8

7 **Corner Option 1:** Turn the corner and glue the next strip of paper, overlapping the corner edge as you did in Step 4. Instead of trimming the excess paper straight along the guideline, miter the corner by trimming the paper diagonally. Align the straight edge with the inside corner and the outside corner and carefully cut the excess paper away with a craft knife (Figure 5-9 and 5-9 detail).

5-9

5-9 detail

Continue applying glue and smoothing the paper in sections until all the strips are glued and the border is complete.

Corner Option 2: For borders that are difficult to match, such as this Greek key, you might want to paint the corners a solid color or use a complementing motif in the corner and run the border paper between the corners (Figure 5-10).

5-10

PAPER NAPKINS & TISSUE PAPER

Thin papers such as paper napkins and tissue paper produce fabulous effects and innovative designs. The papers can be cut into small pieces to create mosaic tile, used as decorative borders, or glued individually as cut shapes. Unlike copy paper or wallpaper, these papers can be overlapped during the gluing process without the worry of excess bulk and paper build-up. However, because of their fragile nature, these thin materials require careful handling.

Use only the printed top layer of a paper napkin or one sheet of tissue paper. Rip them into small irregular shapes approximately 2" (if the piece is too big, the paper will stretch and tear when glued to the canvas). Most printed tissue paper and napkins are bleed-proof, but some solid colored tissue paper isn't, so be sure to test it by gluing several pieces to a piece of poster board before applying to your canvas.

MATERIALS

- ∾ *Paper napkins or tissue paper (I used napkins - "Classic Scroll Arabesque Classique" by Amscan, Inc.)*
- ∾ *Mod Podge or white glue*
- ∾ *Water*
- ∾ *Small mixing container*
- ∾ *Medium size flat artist's brush*
- ∾ *Straight edge*
- ∾ *Tape*
- ∾ *Craft knife*
- ∾ *Pencil*

---

1 Apply two coats of background latex paint to the canvas. Let dry between coats. Tear the paper into irregular jagged shapes

approximately 2". Thin the glue (2 parts glue, 1 part water) in a mixing cup. If you want straight edges (such as a border), pencil the guidelines on the canvas and tape off the edges with painter's masking tape (Figure 5-11).

2 Place a piece of torn napkin or tissue paper on the canvas with a portion of it overlapping the tape. Using the flat artist's brush, apply the glue mixture *over* the paper, carefully smoothing it from the center out. The paper will absorb the glue from the top, sealing it to the canvas. It's normal for the paper to stretch and wrinkle a bit. Cover several inches along the tape.

3 Continue to overlap and glue pieces until the entire area is completed (Figure 5-12). Let dry overnight.

5-12

4 Using a sharp craft knife and straight edge, carefully cut along the taped border to separate the tape from the paper (Figure 5-13). *Don't pull the tape off without cutting it first—it will pull the paper away from the canvas.* Gently and carefully remove the tape.

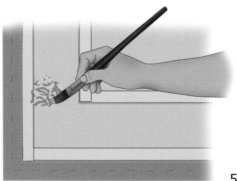

5-11

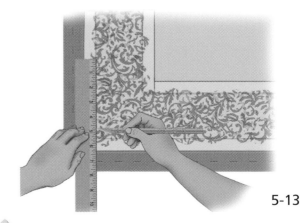

5-13

FABRIC APPLIQUÉ

Various fabrics suitable for decorative application. Top to bottom: 100% cotton decorator chintz (polished cotton) large floral, 100% cotton calico miniprint, and children's motif.

materials such as tapestry, upholstery fabrics, knits, or blends—they're too bulky and won't adhere well to the canvas.

When planning your design, keep in mind that small designs 6"-8" in size are easier to handle and stick to the canvas better than large ones, so use several small cutouts (such as a grouping of flowers or leaves) rather than one large motif. Unlike tissue or paper napkins, fabric doesn't wear well when overlapped during the gluing process, so be sure to plan the design for the motifs to stand alone or be pieced next to each other.

Try to match the background paint to the background of the fabric.

Fabric appliqué is a great way to create interesting color and pattern combinations. Like paper decoupage floorcloths, fabric appliqué floorcloths require a bit more care. Choose from the many lightweight fabrics available today and you will be on your way to creating a unique and exciting floor covering.

The fabrics most suitable for fabric appliqué are 100% cotton calico, 100% cotton decorator-weight chintz (polished cotton), polyester voile, or chiffon. Avoid heavy

SECRETS FOR SUCCESS

∿ *Cut fabric appliqués no larger than 8" and avoid overlapping.*
∿ *If air pockets occur in the appliqué after drying, simply slit the fabric with a craft knife and glue and burnish again.*

Use a lively fabric such as this Concord Seed Packet to adorn the center of a bold checkered border. The fabric is cut into single motifs and glued to the canvas as fabric appliqués. Courtesy of CONCORD Fabrics, pattern # 4106, color XNL.

❶ With a 4" sponge brush or roller, paint the floorcloth with two coats of background color to match the background of the fabric motifs. Let dry between coats. Trim the fabric appliqués with sharp scissors.

❷ Apply a thin line of no-fray glue to all the cut edges of the appliqué (Figure 5-14). Let dry.

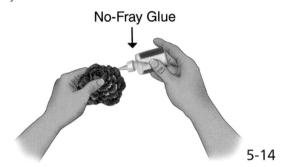

No-Fray Glue

5-14

❸ Determine where you want each of the appliqués on the canvas. Apply an even coat of Mod Podge on the wrong side of one fabric appliqué with the 2" sponge brush (Figure 5-15a). Brush glue on the area of the canvas where the motif will be glued (Figure 5-15b).

Glue

5-15a

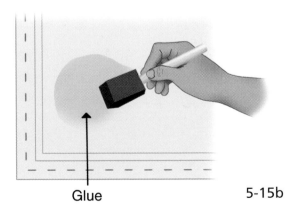

Glue

5-15b

❹ Place the appliqué on the canvas over the glue. Moving from the center to the outside, smooth away any air pockets, wrinkles, and excess glue with the putty knife (Figure 5-16). Wipe away the excess glue with a paper towel. Glue all the appliqués in the same manner and let the fabric dry completely.

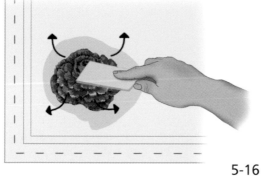

5-16

❺ Lightly sand the appliqué with fine-grade sandpaper or a sanding block to remove any rough fibers (Figure 5-17). Wipe away the sanding residue with a tack cloth and let dry. Brush a coat of glue over the appliqué to seal it, let dry, and sand again.

5-17

(Below) A mixture of paper, paint, and fabric make up this unique "Animal Escapades" floorcloth. I used Animal Fabric #1179B "In the Beginning," courtesy of Alexander Henry Fabrics and Tree Fabric #9147, Hunter, courtesy of Hoffman Fabrics.

Section II: Projects

CHAPTER 6:
SIMPLE FLOORCLOTH PROJECTS

The following floorcloth projects are simple to make—requiring little artistic ability and short working time. They are made with a variety of decorating styles, patterns, and designs which you can embellish with paper decoupage, checkered borders, fabric appliqué, or freehand painting. Refer to Chapters 4 and 5 for detailed information on the techniques used.

Refer to the instructions in Chapter 3 for Basic Floorcloth Construction, Sealing Your Floorcloth, and Hemming the Edges.

ORNAMENTAL TILE

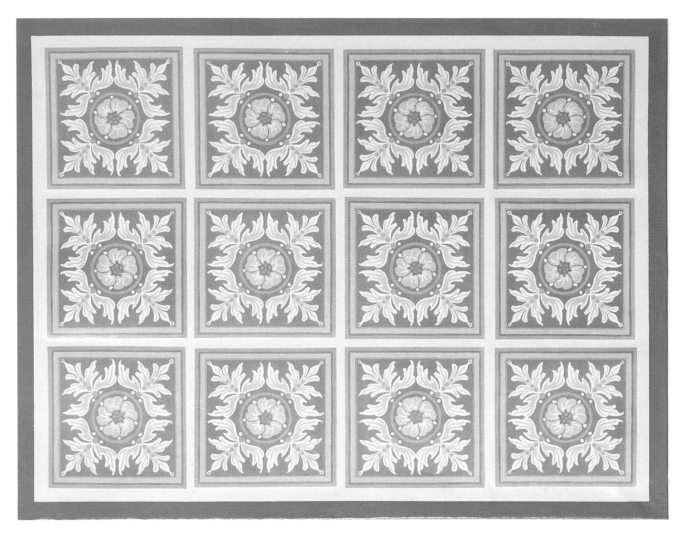

This distinctive floorcloth design is made of decorative paper tiles and a simple solid border. Simply make 12 color copies of the colored tile template provided, paint the border to match, and decoupage the tiles in place to create t h i s sophisticated and timeless work of art. A black and white tile template is also included if you want to create your own color scheme. If you choose to color the tiles yourself, make 12 copies of the black and white tile template and paint them with acrylic paints of your choice before gluing them to the canvas (if you have access to a color photocopier, you can paint just one black and white copy and copy it 12 times).

Finished size: 27" x 35"
Technique: taping, paper decoupage, painting

∾ *Canvas 39" x 31"*
∾ *Stretchers and hardware if needed*
∾ *12 color copies of tile design provided (enlarge tile template to 7½" square)*
∾ *Paint:*
  background—light taupe exterior latex house paint to match lightest taupe in tiles
  border—acrylic paint to match coral in tiles
(Note: If painting your own tiles, use acrylic paints in coral, pale green, light taupe, and dark taupe.)
∾ *Brushes:*
  1" sponge brush
  2 4" sponge brushes
∾ *Plastic putty knife or craft stick for burnishing*
∾ *Scissors*

∾ *Painter's masking tape*
∾ *Craft knife*
∾ *Pencil*
∾ *Metal ruler*
∾ *Paper towel*
∾ *Palette*
∾ *Mod Podge glue or wallpaper adhesive*
∾ *Rubber cement or hot glue gun for hemming*
∾ *1 qt. water-based clear sealer, varnish, or polyurethane in matte or satin finish*

Colors shown in photo:
Background: Benjamin Moore MooreGard latex house paint #944
Tiles: DecoArt Americana acrylic paints in Gooseberry DA27, Green Mist DA177, Buttermilk DA3, Titanium (Snow) White DA1, Cool Neutral (toning) DA89

Cut Size 39" x 31"
Finished Size 35" x 27"

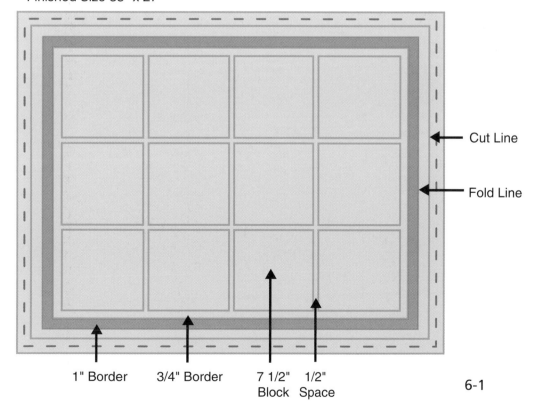

Cut Line

Fold Line

1" Border   3/4" Border   7 1/2" Block   1/2" Space

6-1

TECHNIQUE

❶ Stretch the canvas on a flat or open stretcher, following the instructions in Chapter 3.

❷ Apply two coats of background color to the canvas with a 4" sponge brush or roller. Let dry between coats.

❸ Refer to Figure 6-1 and pencil in the cut line, fold line, 1" border line, and tile placement guidelines.

❹ Tape off both sides of the 1" border, burnishing the edges of the tape well (Figure 6-2).

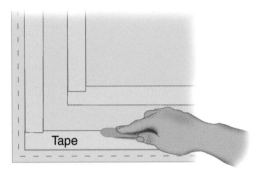

Tape

6-2

❺ Using a 1" sponge brush, paint in the border, being careful not to push paint under the tape (Figure 6-3). Let dry and apply a second coat.

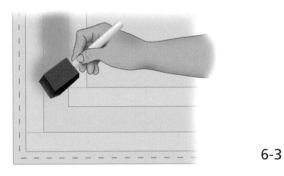

6-3

❻ Using a craft knife and straight edge, trim the edges of the 12 paper tiles (Figure 6-4).

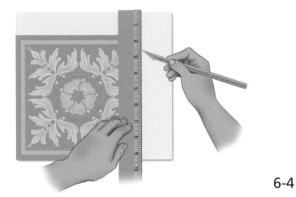

6-4

❼ Use a sponge brush to apply an even coat of Mod Podge or wallpaper adhesive to the back of a paper tile (Figure 6-5).

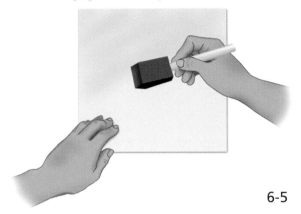

6-5

❽ Follow the instructions for Decoupage Cutouts on page 49 to glue a paper tile inside a block on the canvas. Using a plastic putty knife, smooth the paper from the center to the outside edges to expel any excess glue and air bubbles (Figure 6-6).

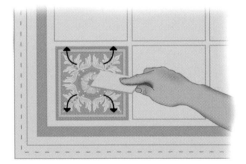

6-6

Wipe away any glue left on the canvas after each pass. Glue on all the paper tiles in this manner and let dry overnight.

❾ Follow the instructions in Chapter 3 for Sealing your Floorcloth and Hemming the Edges.

ORNAMENTAL TILE TEMPLATES

SWIRLS, CURLS & WAVES

This floorcloth is fast, fun, and simple to make. The design is versatile and fits in a variety of decorating styles including classical, contemporary, or juvenile, depending on the color scheme. I used paint pens, but markers or watered down acrylic paints in a squeeze bottle would work just as well.

Finished size: 40" x 36"
Technique: freehand designs with paint pens

MATERIALS	

∾ Canvas 44" x 40"
 ∾ Stretchers
 ∾ Paint:
    background—black exterior latex
      house paint
 ∾ 4" sponge brush
 ∾ Gold and white paint pens
 ∾ White pencil or chalk
	∾ 1 qt. water-based clear sealer,
	    polyurethane, or varnish
	    in matte or satin finish
	 ∾ Rubber cement or hot glue gun for
	    hemming
	
	 Colors shown in photo:
	 Background: Benjamin Moore MooreGard latex house
	 paint # 80

Cut Size 44" x 40"
Finished Size 40" x 36"

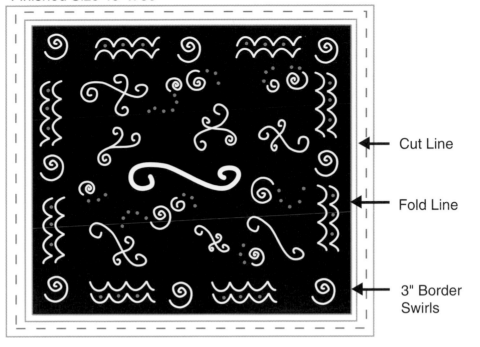

← Cut Line

← Fold Line

← 3" Border
Swirls

6-7

TECHNIQUE

❶ Stretch the canvas on a flat or open stretcher, following the instructions in Chapter 3.

❷ Using a 4" sponge brush or roller, apply two coats of black background color to the canvas. Let dry between coats.

❸ Refer to Figure 6-7 and the project photo and pencil in the design with a white pencil or chalk.

❹ Trace over each swirl, curl, and wave with a white paint pen. Two coats may be necessary, depending upon how heavily the paint goes on. Let dry between each coat (Figure 6-8).

❺ Using a gold pen, apply dots on the end of the swirls and between the waves (Figure 6-9).

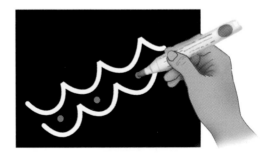

6-9

❻ Follow the instructions in Chapter 3 for Sealing Your Floorcloth and Hemming the Edges.

6-8

CIRCLE OF STARS

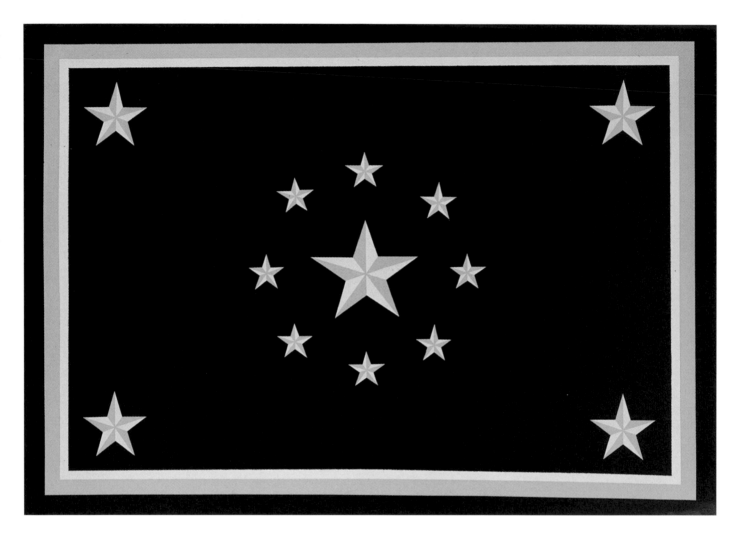

Add this distinctive floorcloth design to your traditional, country, or eclectic decor. The versatile design and color scheme coordinates with an array of styles and accessories. Both color and black and white templates are provided to make the paper decoupage stars. Or you can hand-paint, stencil, or stamp on the stars to vary the overall texture and appearance.

Finished size: 50" x 36"
Technique: painting, taping, paper decoupage

MATERIALS

- ∾ *Canvas 54" x 40"*
- ∾ *Stretchers*
- ∾ *Paint:*
  background—red exterior latex
  house paint
  stars and border—yellow
  acrylic paint (or use color
  copies of the colored star
  template provided)
- ∾ *Brushes:*
  2" sponge paint brush
  4" sponge paint brush or roller
- ∾ *Designs (enlarge or reduce the*
  template as needed):
  1 7" center star
  4 4½" corner stars
  8 2½" circle stars
- ∾ *Mod Podge glue or wallpaper*
  border adhesive

- ∾ *Plastic putty knife or craft stick*
  for burnishing
- ∾ *Artist's gum or plastic eraser*
- ∾ *Ruler*
- ∾ *Craft knife*
- ∾ *White marking pencil*
- ∾ *Painter's masking tape*
- ∾ *Rubber cement or hot glue gun for*
  hemming
- ∾ *1 qt. water-based clear sealer,*
  varnish, or polyurethane in
  matte or satin finish

Colors shown in photo:
Background: Benjamin Moore MooreGard latex house paint, Heritage Red #09625
Stars: DecoArt Americana acrylic paint in Moon Yellow DA7

SECRETS FOR SUCCESS

∾ *After copying the first two stars, cut and paste several stars on one page to reduce copy costs.*

TECHNIQUE

1 Stretch the canvas on a flat stretcher or open frame, following the instructions in Chapter 3.

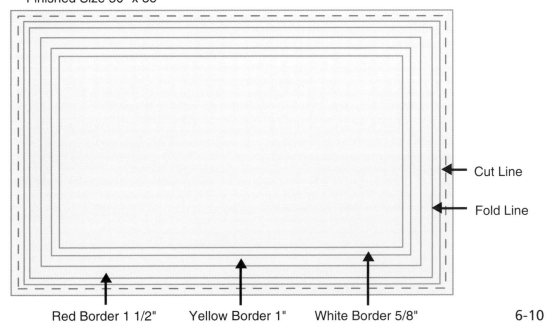

Cut Size 54" x 40"
Finished Size 50" x 36"

Cut Line

Fold Line

Red Border 1 1/2"   Yellow Border 1"   White Border 5/8"   6-10

❷ Refer to Figure 6-10 and draw the cut line, fold line, and borders around the perimeter of the canvas. Cover the designated white and yellow borders with painter's masking tape and burnish the tape edges well with a craft stick or putty knife.

❸ Using a 4" sponge brush or roller, paint the background with two coats of red. Let dry thoroughly between coats. A third coat may be necessary, depending on the coverage of the first two. When the last coat of paint is tacky, remove the tape and let the paint dry thoroughly.

❹ Apply tape on the outside of the designated yellow border, burnish the edges of the tape well, and apply two coats of yellow (Figure 6-11) with the 2" sponge brush. Let dry between coats. When the last coat is tacky, remove the tape. The white background will make up the white border.

6-11

❺ Using a white pencil, find and mark the center of the floorcloth. Draw a 14" circle around it and divide the circle first into 1/4 sections and then into 1/8 sections (Figure 6-12).

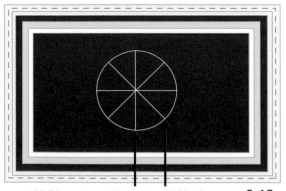

14" Diameter   1/4 Mark   1/8 Mark   6-12

❻ Trim the excess paper away from each of the paper stars with a craft knife and straight edge (Figure 6-13).

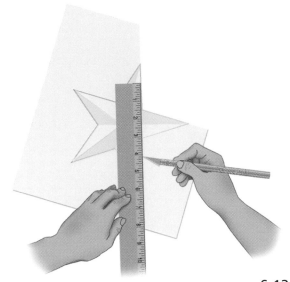

6-13

❼ Follow the instructions for Decoupage Cutouts on page 49 to glue the stars in place. Glue the large center star first, followed by the small stars circling it. Line up the center of each star with the 1/4 and 1/8 section lines. Finish by gluing the corner stars 1" from the white border. Be sure to apply enough glue to the paper and burnish the motifs well (Figure 6-14).

6-14

❽ Erase any white lines and touch up areas as needed with red background paint.

❾ Follow the instructions in Chapter 3 for Sealing Your Floorcloth and Hemming the Edges.

STAR TEMPLATES

Enlarge or reduce to project specifications.

CONTEMPORARY CRESCENTS

Create a refreshing contemporary floorcloth with this unique painting technique. The streaked appearance is done by *drybrushing*—removing most of the paint from the brush before applying it to the canvas.

Stretch a rectangular piece of canvas instead of the semicircular shape to make the stretching and working process easier. Draw the semicircular shape on the rectangle and cut it out after varnishing.

Finished size: 36" semicircle
Technique: freehand designs, painting

MATERIALS
～ *Canvas 40" x 22" (rectangle)*   ～ *Paper towels*

∾ *Canvas 40" x 22" (rectangle)*
∾ *Stretchers*
∾ *Paint:*
   background—white exterior latex
     house paint
   crescents—acrylic paints in green,
     mauve, blue, yellow
∾ *Brushes:*
   1/2" flat artist's brush
   1" bristle brush
   2" bristle brush
   4" sponge brush
∾ *Pencil*
∾ *Ruler*

∾ *Paper towels*
∾ *Painter's tape*
∾ *Craft knife*
∾ *Small mixing cup*
∾ *Rubber cement or hot glue gun for*
   hemming
∾ *1 qt. water-based clear sealer,*
   varnish, or polyurethane in
   matte or satin finish

Colors shown in photo:
Background: Benjamin Moore MooreGard latex house paint #01
Crescents: DecoArt Americana acrylic paints in Colonial Green DA81, French Mauve DA186, Uniform Blue DA86, Moon Yellow DA7

Cut Size 40" x 22"
Finished Size 36" x 18"

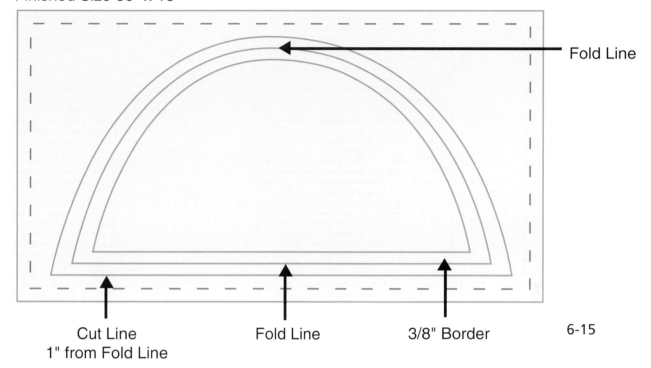

Fold Line

Cut Line
1" from Fold Line

Fold Line

3/8" Border

6-15

TECHNIQUE

❶ Stretch the canvas on a flat or open stretcher, following the instructions in Chapter 3.

❷ Using a 4" sponge brush or roller, apply two coats of white paint on the canvas. Let dry between coats.

❸ Refer to Figure 6-15 and lightly pencil in the cut line, fold line, and border line. For better control, you may want to lightly draw in the crescent placement, following the pattern in the photo.

❹ Using the 1/2" flat artist's brush, paint in the green border. You can paint it freehand (Figure 6-16) or tape it with painter's masking tape stretched and slit to fit along the curve (Figure 6-17). Apply only one coat so it will look streaked like the texture in the crescent shapes.

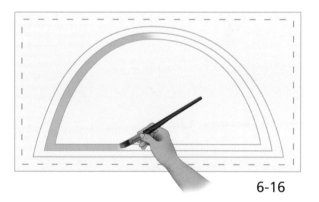

6-16

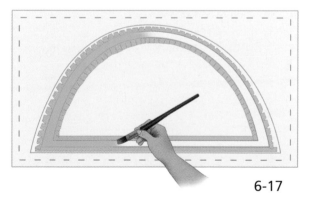

6-17

❺ Refer to the instructions for painting Crescents on page 29 and paint in the design. Use the green, mauve, and yellow paints straight from the bottle and dilute the blue with two or three drops of white in a small mixing cup. Use a 2" bristle brush for the large green and blue crescents and a 1" bristle brush for the smaller mauve and yellow crescents (Figure 6-18). Allow each color to dry completely before applying the next one.

❻ Follow the instructions in Chapter 3 for Sealing Your Floorcloth and Hemming the Edges.

6-18

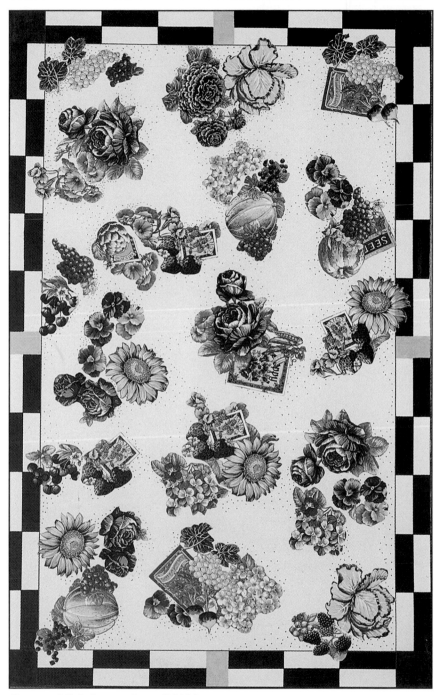

Finished size: 47" x 30"
Technique: fabric appliqué, painted checkered border

Concord Fabrics, pattern #4106

Checkered borders are timeless patterns that can be paired with a variety of decorative applications. Here the border is combined with a bright 100% cotton calico fabric cut into individual flower, fruit, and vegetable motifs and decoupaged to the canvas. Use a single fabric or several coordinating fabrics to jazz up your floorcloth design and enhance its surroundings.

MATERIALS

- Canvas 51" x 34"
- 1 yd. lightweight fabric
  (I used Concord, pattern #4106)
- Paint:
  background—white exterior latex
    house paint
  border designs—acrylic paints in
    black, orange, and red to match
    the paint pens or markers
- Black, orange, red, and royal
    blue paint pens or permanent
    markers
- Brushes:
  medium size flat artist's brush
  2" sponge paint brush
  4" sponge paint brush or roller
- Ruler
- Scissors

- Plastic putty knife or craft stick
    for burnishing
- Mod Podge glue or other fabric
    glue
- Painter's masking tape
- Paper towels
- Pencil
- Rubber cement or hot glue gun
    for hemming
- 1 qt. water-based acrylic sealer,
    varnish, or polyurethane in
    matte or satin finish

Colors shown in photo:
Background: Benjamin Moore MooreGard latex house paint #01
Designs: DecoArt Americana acrylic paints in Marigold DA194, Primary Red DA199, Lamp Black DA67

Cut Size 51" x 34"
Finished Size 47" x 30"

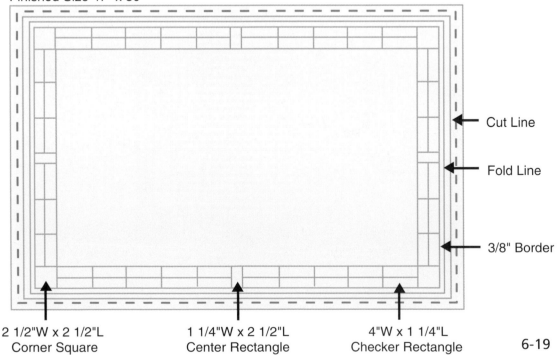

Cut Line

Fold Line

3/8" Border

2 1/2"W x 2 1/2"L
Corner Square

1 1/4"W x 2 1/2"L
Center Rectangle

4"W x 1 1/4"L
Checker Rectangle

6-19

❶ Stretch the canvas on a flat or open stretcher, following the instructions in Chapter 3.

❷ Use a 4" sponge brush or roller to apply two coats of white background color, letting the first coat dry before applying the second.

❸ Refer to Figure 6-19 and pencil in the cut line, fold line, checkered border, corner squares, and center border rectangle.

❹ Refer to the instructions for Checkered Borders on page 33 and outline the black boxes using a black paint pen. Let dry. Using the flat artist's brush, fill in the boxes with black acrylic paint. Repeat for the orange rectangles, outlining them with an orange paint pen and filling the rectangle with orange. Outline the red corner squares with a red paint pen and fill them in with red. Let dry.

❺ Using a straight edge and paint pens or markers, draw in a 1/4″ blue line on the inside of the checkered boxes and a 3/8″ red border on the outside of the boxes (Figure 6-20).

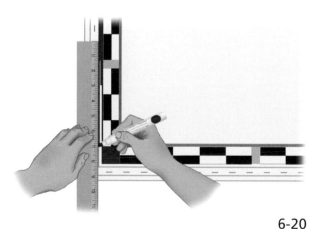

6-20

❻ Refer to the instructions for Fabric Appliqué on page 55. Trim the fabric motifs, apply no-fray glue, and glue them to the canvas. Burnish each appliqué well, especially the edges, to ensure adequate sealing (Figure 6-21).

6-21

❼ Using the same blue paint pen as in the border, randomly apply dots around the perimeters of the fabric motifs as shown in Figure 6-21 and the photo below. Let dry thoroughly.

❽ Follow the instructions in Chapter 3 for Sealing Your Floorcloth and Hemming the Edges.

RAINBOW HOPSCOTCH

Bring outdoor games inside with this multi-colored hopscotch floorcloth. It has a rainbow of colors and a road for cars too! Apply the design with acrylic paints and a paint pen. It's fast, simple, and takes little or no artistic ability.

Finished size:
30" x 54½"

Technique:
painting, taping,
paint pens or markers

TECHNIQUE

① Stretch the canvas on a flat or open stretcher, following the instructions in Chapter 3.

② Refer to Figure 6-22 and draw in the cut line, fold line, hopscotch blocks, and road.

③ If you feel comfortable with freehand painting, you can paint the hopscotch blocks freehand. If not, tape them off with painter's masking tape. Apply tape to every other block and burnish well (Figure 6-23). Using a separate 2" sponge brush for each color, apply two coats of paint to the four taped off areas. Let dry between coats. Some colors may require a third coat depending on the coverage of the paint. Remove the tape when the last coat of each color is tacky and clean the brushes. Let dry thoroughly.

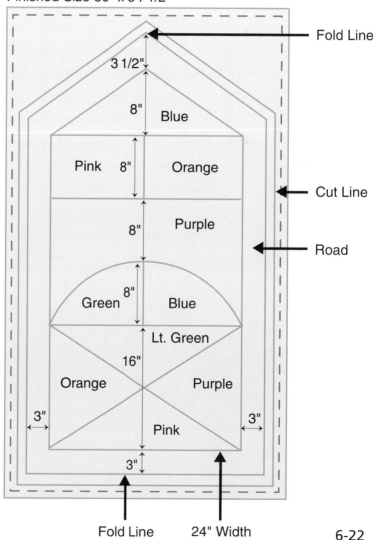

Cut Size 34" x 60"
Finished Size 30" x 54 1/2"

Fold Line

3 1/2"

8" Blue

Pink 8" Orange

Cut Line

8" Purple

Road

Green 8" Blue

Lt. Green

16" Orange Purple

3" 3"

Pink

3"

Fold Line 24" Width

6-22

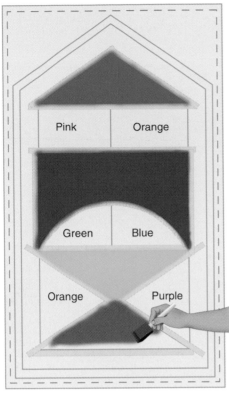

6-23

4 Tape off, burnish, and paint all remaining areas except the left pink square and the left green quarter circle (Figure 6-24). Let dry and remove the tape. Tape off and paint the pink square and green quarter circle. Let dry thoroughly.

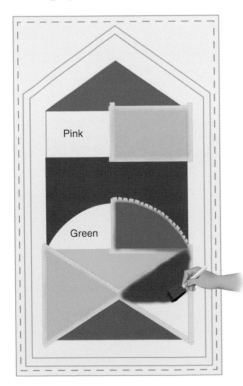

6-24

5 Tape off, burnish, and apply two coats of paint to the black road (Figure 6-25). Let dry and remove the tape.

6-25

6 Using a white pencil or chalk, draw in the block numbers and median lines for the road. Trace over each number and line with a white paint pen (Figure 6-26).

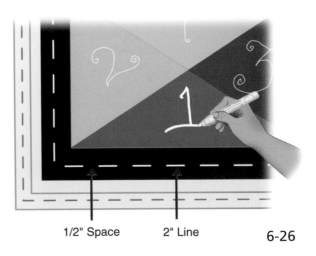

1/2" Space   2" Line   **6-26**

7 Follow the instructions in Chapter 3 for Sealing Your Floorcloth and Hemming the Edges.

CLASSICAL TABLE RUNNER

Grace your table with this sophisticated table runner reminiscent of days gone by. It's created with a set of black and white copies and some very simple paint techniques that enhance and accent the elegant figures. Use the templates provided or a favorite design of your own to make your table a special showcase for your family and friends to admire.

This project is painted on sign cloth, a lightweight synthetic canvas suitable for areas where moisture is a consideration but frequent wear is not.

Finished size: 26" x 14"
Technique: paper decoupage, taping, painting

SECRETS FOR SUCCESS

∾ *To avoid having to cut out tiny areas on the figures, paint intricate areas in and around the figures to match the background color they sit on.*

Black and white photocopies are used as the primary decorative medium in this paper decoupage table runner.

- *30" x 18" sign cloth or lightweight primed canvas (I used Taracloth by Fredrix)*
- *Stretchers*
- *Black and white photocopies: 2 of each figure, 6 urns*
- *Acrylic paints in cream, teal green, holly green, white*
- *Brushes:*
  small pointed artist's brush
  2" sponge brush
  4" sponge brush
- *Mod Podge or wallpaper adhesive*
- *Painter's masking tape*
- *Pencil*

- *Ruler*
- *Craft knife*
- *Craft stick or plastic putty knife for burnishing*
- *Paper towels*
- *Mixing cups*
- *Rubber cement or hot glue gun for hemming*
- *1 qt. water-based acrylic sealer, varnish, or polyurethane in matte or satin finish*

Colors shown in photo:
DecoArt Americana acrylics: Buttermilk DA3, Teal Green DA107, Holly Green DA48, Snow White DA1

TECHNIQUE

❶ Stretch the canvas on a flat or open stretcher, following the instructions in Chapter 3.

❷ Refer to Figure 6-27 and draw in the cut line, fold line, curved corner lines, and center rectangle.

❸ Tape off the center rectangle, burnishing

Cut Size 30" x 18"
Finished Size 26" x 14"

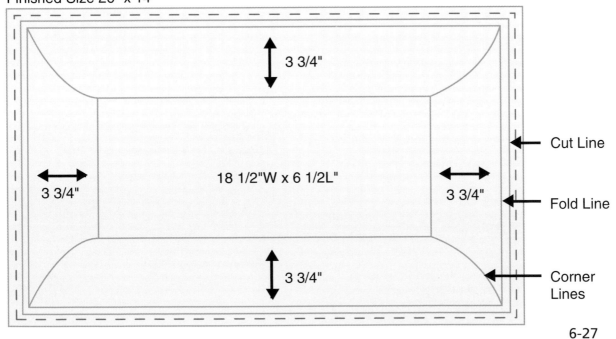

3 3/4"

3 3/4"

18 1/2"W x 6 1/2L"

3 3/4"

3 3/4"

Cut Line

Fold Line

Corner Lines

6-27

the tape well. Using a 4" sponge brush, apply one uneven coat of cream paint, creating a somewhat streaked weathered effect (Figure 6-28). Let dry and remove the tape.

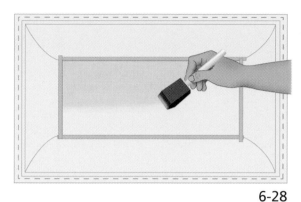

6-28

4 Tape off both teal green areas and burnish the tape well, bending and slitting the tape to conform to the curved line (Figure 6-29).

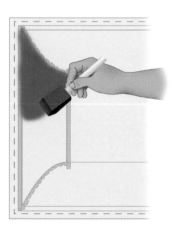

6-29

5 Mix three parts teal green with one part white in a small mixing cup. Using a 2" sponge brush, apply two coats of the paint mixture inside the taped area. Let dry between coats and remove the tape after the second coat is tacky.

6 Repeat on the two long sides, applying a mixture of three parts holly green and one part white.

7 Make black and white copies of the figures and urn templates provided. Prepare and glue the cutouts in place, following the Decoupage Cutout instructions on page 49.

8 Using a small pointed artist's brush, apply four thin "L" shaped lines in each corner of the center rectangle with the holly green mixture. The longest line is 1¼" long and each subsequent line is 1/8" shorter (Figure 6-30).

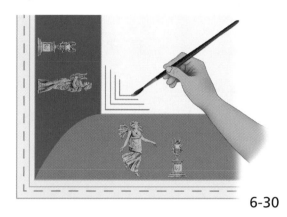

6-30

9 Refer to Figure 6-31 and pencil in the striped peaks around the perimeter of each side. Using the small pointed artist's brush, paint cream lines to create the peaks (Figure 6-32).

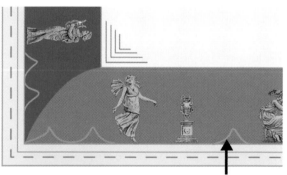

6-31   Peak Guidelines

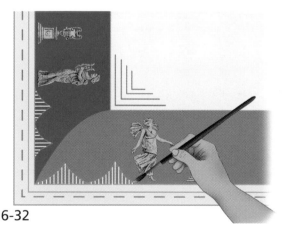

6-32

10 Follow the instructions in Chapter 3 for Sealing Your Floorcloth and Hemming the Edges.

CLASSICAL TABLE RUNNER TEMPLATES

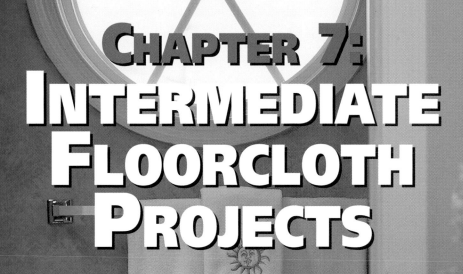

CHAPTER 7:
INTERMEDIATE FLOORCLOTH PROJECTS

The projects in this chapter are slightly more complicated and require a higher level of artistic skill and additional working time. Choose from projects such as a stamped brick garden, contrasting white and black faux marble, a welcome mat, or an intricate lace design. Follow the easy step-by-step instructions to create an inspiring work of art you will treasure.

Bring a bit of sunshine indoors with this charming garden view floorcloth. The brick pattern is created with everyday kitchen sponges stamped in alternating colors to make them appear more realistic. Precut rubber stamps imprint the variety of fern leaves. Because the leaf shapes are so genuine looking, they create a flowing combination of color, pattern, and texture around the geometric center design.

Finished size: 48" x 36"
Technique: stamping, sponging

SECRETS FOR SUCCESS

∾ *Baby wipes clean rubber stamps quickly and easily.*
∾ *Place the stamps in a bowl of water while working with other colors and to make cleanup easier when finished.*

- *Canvas 52" x 40"*
- *Stretchers*
- *Plaid Decorator Blocks, Fern Variety #53237*
- *Paint:*
  background—tan exterior latex house paint
  designs—acrylic paints in jade green, antique green, forest green, terra cotta, blue, mocha, flesh
- *Brushes:*
  4" sponge brush or roller
  medium size flat artist's brush
  small round artist's brush
- *2 flat rectangular cellulose kitchen sponges approximately 4"-6" in size*

- *Paper plates*
- *Ruler*
- *Pencil*
- *Paper towels*
- *Baby wipes*
- *Rubber cement or hot glue gun for hemming*
- *1 qt. water-based acrylic sealer, varnish, or polyurethane in matte or satin finish*
- *Bowl of water*

Colors shown in photo:
Background: Benjamin Moore MooreGard latex house paint #969
Designs: DecoArt Americana acrylics in Jade Green DA57, Antique Green DA147, Forest Green DA50, Terra Cotta DA62, Country Blue DA41, Mocha DA60, Shading Flesh DA137

TECHNIQUE

❶ Stretch the canvas on a flat or open stretcher, following the instructions in Chapter 3.

❷ Apply one coat of background color to the canvas with a 4" sponge brush or roller. Let dry.

❸ Pencil in the cut line, fold line, and brick border line (Figure 7-1).

Cut Size 52" x 40"
Finished Size 48" x 36"

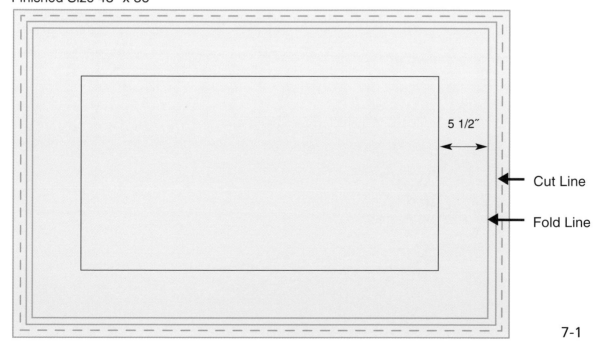

5 1/2″

Cut Line

Fold Line

7-1

4 To create the stamped brick motif, follow the instructions for Brick Paving on page 39. You will use three different colors of paint for the brick stamps. Pour some mocha and terra cotta on one paper plate, and some mocha and flesh on another paper plate. Use a different sponge for each paint combination and alternate the colors to create a realistic effect (Figure 7-2).

7-2

5 Each size fern is stamped with one or two colors. The large leaf stamp is forest green mixed with a bit of antique green. The medium leaf is antique green and the small leaf is jade green. Begin with the large leaf stamp. You can create more shading by applying several shades of color on the stamp simultaneously. Apply a light coat of paint to the stamp using a flat artist's brush and press it firmly on the canvas. Carefully lift off and stamp again in a different place without repainting the stamp (Figure 7-3). Refer to the stamping instructions on page 37.

7-3

6 Repeat the process using the medium and small leaf stamps, intermingling and overlapping them to create varied shading and a layered appearance (Figure 7-4).

7-4

7 Using a small round artist's brush, paint in the small blue flowers randomly for added detail and color (Figure 7-5).

7-5

8 Follow the instructions in Chapter 3 for Sealing Your Floorcloth and Hemming the Edges.

WHITE & BLACK MARBLE

Create this fabulous faux marble floorcloth with a quick and easy veining technique, striking black diamonds, and a black and gold border. The diamonds are paper decoupage but you could stencil, stamp, or hand paint them too. To create realistic veining, practice on poster board before working on the canvas.

Finished size: 48" x 26"
Technique: veining, taping, paper decoupage

MATERIALS

- Canvas 52" x 30"
- Stretchers
- Paint:
  background—white exterior
    latex house paint
  designs—acrylic paints in light
    grey, medium grey, dark grey,
    black, metallic gold
- Copies: 1 large motif for the
    center, 6 medium diamonds, 2
    small diamonds
- Brushes:
  1" sponge brush
  2" sponge brush
  4" sponge brush or roller
  2" soft bristle brush for
    blending
- Pointed feather (not dyed)
- Paint pens or markers (black
    and metallic gold)

- Artist's fixative for paint pens or
    markers if not permanent
- Painter's masking tape
- Pencil
- Scissors
- Craft knife
- Ruler
- Craft stick or putty knife for
    burnishing
- Rubber cement or hot glue gun
    for hemming
- Cotton rag
- 1 qt. water-based acrylic sealer,
    varnish, or polyurethane in
    matte or satin finish

Colors shown in photo:
Background: Benjamin Moore MooreGard latex house paint #01
Designs: DecoArt Americana acrylics in Dove Grey DA69, Neutral Grey (toning) DA95, Graphite DA161, Lamp (Ebony) Black DA67, Dazzling Metallics Glorious Gold DA71

TECHNIQUE

1 Stretch the canvas on a flat or open stretcher, following the instructions in Chapter 3.

2 Apply two coats of white paint to the canvas with a 4" sponge brush or roller. Let dry between coats.

3 Refer to Figure 7-6 and draw in the cut line, fold line, and black and gold borders.

Cut Size 52" x 30"
Finished Size 48" x 26"

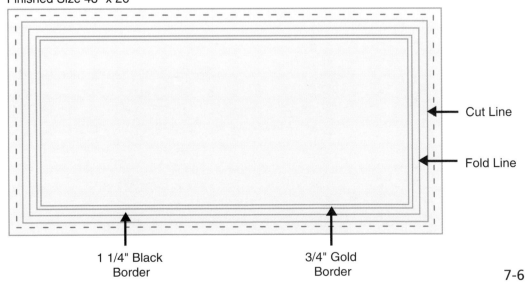

Cut Line

Fold Line

1 1/4" Black Border

3/4" Gold Border

7-6

❹ Tape off the outside and inside edges of the gold border and burnish the tape securely. Apply two coats of gold paint with the 1" sponge brush between the tape, letting the paint dry between coats (Figure 7-7). Remove the tape and let dry thoroughly. Repeat for the black border. Let dry.

7-7

❺ Follow the instructions for Veining on page 44 to create the central white and black marbled finish. Let dry. See Figure 7-8 for a view of the overall finished effect.

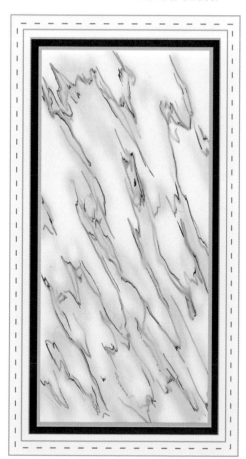

7-8

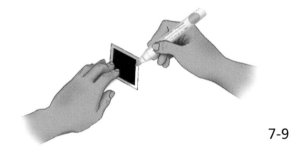

Close up of veining applied with a feather.

❻ Make color copies of the black and gold templates provided. (To paint your own, use the uncolored templates provided. Paint the designated pieces black and draw a 1/8" border around the outside of all the diamonds with a gold paint pen as shown in Figure 7-9. Let dry.)

7-9

❼ Cut out the six medium diamonds, two small diamonds, all the white areas inside the large diamond motif, including the small center diamond which will be glued on separately. Be sure to keep this separated from the other small diamonds.

❽ Refer to Figure 7-10 and mark the canvas for placement of each diamond. Refer to the Decoupage Cutout instructions on page 49 and glue the large diamond motif, the six medium diamonds, and two small diamonds in place. Carefully burnish the cutouts (Figure 7-11). Let dry.

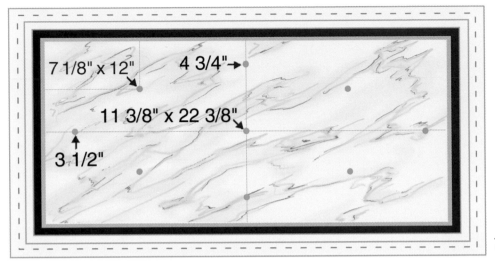

7 1/8" x 12"

4 3/4" →

11 3/8" x 22 3/8"

↑
3 1/2"

7-10

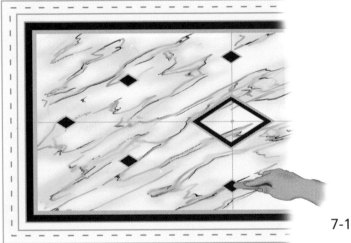

7-11

❾ If you painted the motifs yourself, glue the large center diamond first. Burnish and let dry. Then glue the gold square on top of the diamond, glue the small center diamond inside the square, burnish, and let dry (Figures 7-11 and 7-12).

❿ Follow the instructions in Chapter 3 for Sealing Your Floorcloth and Hemming the Edges.

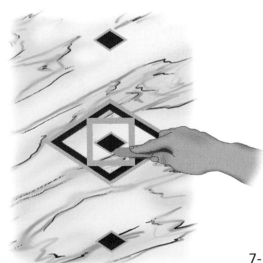

7-12

WHITE & BLACK MARBLE TEMPLATES

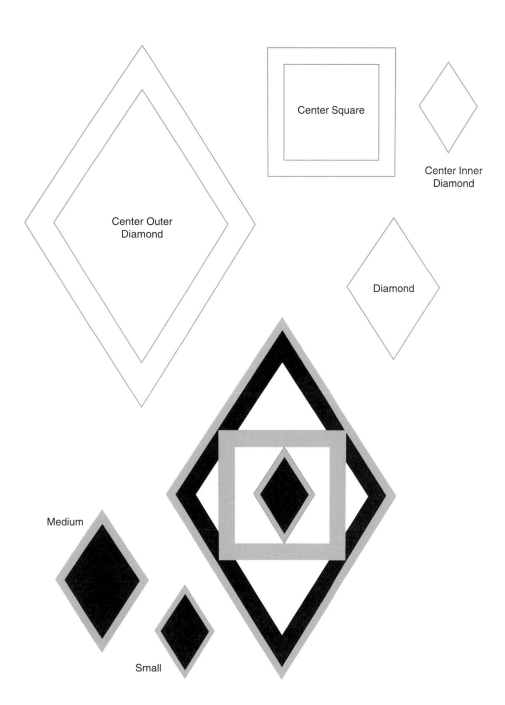

Center Square

Center Inner Diamond

Center Outer Diamond

Diamond

Medium

Small

This welcome mat is certainly not your run-of-the-mill floor covering. Thanks to unique luncheon napkins, plain and simple becomes sophisticated and elegant. This project combines stenciling, paper decoupage, and taping to create the interesting combination of pattern and texture. The paper application requires additional time but the finished result is well worth it.

Finished size: 44" x 29"
Technique: paper decoupage, taping, stenciling

(The napkins used are courtesy of Amscan, Inc. "Classic Scroll, Arabesque Classique" item #51277, RMET96106Q04)

MATERIALS

- *Canvas 48" x 33"*
- *Stretchers*
- *Paint:*
  background—ivory exterior
  latex house paint
  designs—acrylic paints in teal
  green, yellow, khaki tan
- *2 packages napkins with designs*
  of your choice (I used Amscan
  Luncheon Napkin Classic
  Scroll Arabesque Classique
  Item #51277)
- *Welcome stencil #28521 by Plaid*
  Enterprises and a large
  pineapple stencil
- *Brushes:*
  1" sponge brush
  2" sponge brush
  4" sponge brush or roller
  small flat artist's brush

- *small stencil brush*
  medium stencil brush
- *Mod Podge or white glue*
- *Pencil*
- *Ruler*
- *Painter's masking tape*
- *Craft knife*
- *Scissors*
- *Palette*
- *Small mixing cup and water*
- *Rubber cement or hot glue gun*
  for hemming
- *1 qt. water-based acrylic sealer,*
  varnish, or polyurethane in
  matte or satin finish

Colors shown in photo:
Background: Benjamin Moore MooreGard ivory latex house paint #206
Designs: DecoArt Americana acrylic paints in Teal Green DA107, Moon Yellow DA7, Khaki Tan DA173

TECHNIQUE

1 Stretch the canvas on a flat or open stretcher, following the instructions in Chapter 3.

2 Using a 4" sponge brush or roller, apply two coats of ivory to the canvas, letting the paint dry between coats.

3 Refer to Figure 7-13 and pencil in the cut line, fold line, borders, and center rectangle.

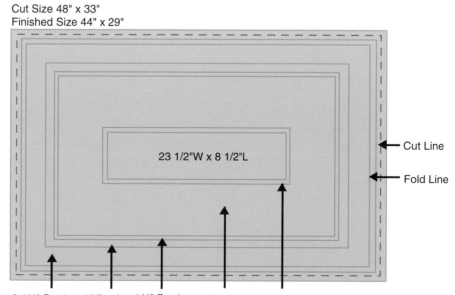

Cut Size 48" x 33"
Finished Size 44" x 29"

23 1/2"W x 8 1/2"L

← Cut Line

← Fold Line

2 1/4" Border   1" Border   1/4" Border   6 3/4" Border   1/4" Border

7-13

4 To paint the green and khaki borders, tape off both sides of the ivory border and inside the designated green borders (Figure 7-14). Burnish the edge of the tape several times to prevent paint from seeping underneath and apply two coats of green and khaki paint. Let dry between coats. Remove the tape

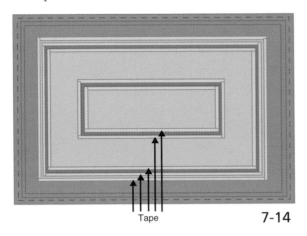

Tape   7-14

5 Follow the instructions for stenciling in Chapter 4 and stencil the "Welcome" in the center rectangle of the canvas, using the medium stencil brush with undiluted teal green paint (Figure 7-15).

7-15

6 Center and secure the pineapple stencil between the green border and the "Welcome" on the left side. Tape off the inside portion of the stencil and use the small stencil brush to paint the pineapple foliage teal green (Figure 7-16). Let dry and clean the brush.

7-16

7 Remove the tape and apply new tape over the green areas on the design. Mix some khaki tan with a small amount of yellow in a mixing cup and stencil the center portion of the pineapple design using the small stencil brush (Figure 7-17). Remove the stencil and repeat the process for the pineapple on the other side.

7-17

8 Separate the layers of the napkin and discard all but the single top printed layer. Cut off the darkest border on each napkin, layer them about 4-5 in a stack, and tear them into pieces approximately 2" in length.

9 Apply tape around the outside edge of the center green border and the inside edge of the outer green border (Figure 7-18). Following the Paper Napkin instructions on page 53, place a piece of napkin over the taped border into the center area and use the flat artist's brush to apply thinned white glue (2 parts glue, 1 part water) over the paper from the middle to the outside. It's normal for the paper to stretch and wrinkle a bit as you work. Continue overlapping the papers and gluing until the entire outside border area is covered with the napkin motif. Let dry overnight.

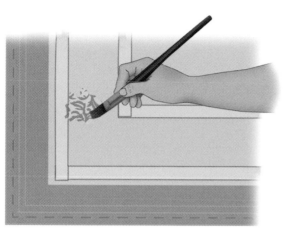

7-18

❿ Using a craft knife and straight edge, carefully cut along the tape line to separate the tape from the paper. This will ensure that the edge of the border is straight (Figure 7-19).

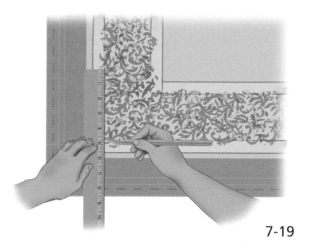

7-19

⓫ Follow the instructions in Chapter 3 for Sealing your Floorcloth and Hemming the Edges.

VICTORIAN LACE

Create the intricate detailing of lace in minutes with the doily spray technique. The lace pattern is made when paper doilies are temporarily secured to the canvas and sprayed with an acrylic water-based spray paint. When the doilies are removed, the complex lace design is left behind. The hand-painted detailing highlights smaller features of the pattern and incorporates additional colors into the floorcloth design. This project requires attention and patience to produce a clean edge and even overall finish.

Finished size:
45" x 26"
Technique:
doily spray,
hand-painted roping

(The "Basket Lace Square" doily used is courtesy of Royal Lace)

- *Canvas 49" x 30"*
- *Stretchers*
- *1 package paper doiles (I used 8" Royal Lace, "Basket Lace Square")*
- *Paint:*
  lace color—ivory exterior latex house paint
  background—royal blue acrylic spray paint
  detailing—acrylic paints in green, mauve, and royal blue to match the background
- *Brushes:*
  medium flat artist's brush
  small round pointed artist's brush for detailing
  4" sponge brush or roller

- *Repositionable spray adhesive*
- *Pencil*
- *Palette*
- *Craft knife*
- *Craft stick or plastic putty knife for burnishing*
- *Rubber cement or hot glue gun for hemming*
- *1 qt. water-based acrylic sealer, varnish, or polyurethane in matte or satin finish*

Colors shown in photo:
Background and doilies: Benjamin Moore MooreGard latex house paint #79
Detailing: DecoArt Americana acrylic paints in Colonial Green DA81, French Mauve DA186

TECHNIQUE

❶ Stretch the canvas on a flat or open stretcher, following the instructions in Chapter 3.

❷ Apply two coats of ivory to the canvas with a 4" sponge brush or roller. Let dry between coats.

❸ Refer to Figure 7-20 and pencil in the cut line, fold line, border line, and center lines.

Cut Size 49" x 30"
Finished Size 45" x 26"

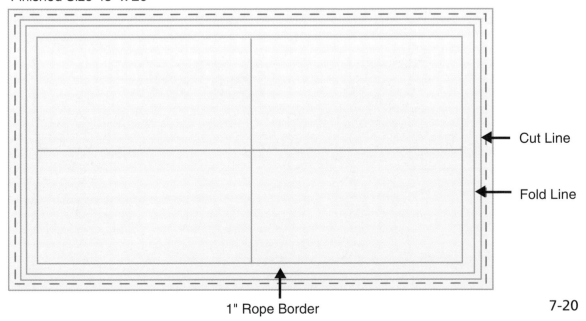

Cut Line

Fold Line

1" Rope Border

7-20

❹ Set aside six full doilies and cut eight doily corners from two other doilies. Cover the roping border area with tape and burnish. Position the doilies on the canvas and lightly trace around them with a pencil. Refer to Figure 7-21 for doily placement.

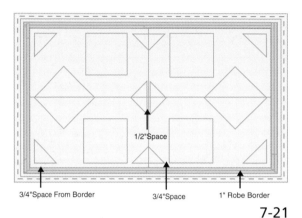

1/2"Space

3/4"Space From Border   3/4"Space   1" Robe Border

7-21

❺ Follow the instructions for the Doily Spray technique on page 40 to create the design. Let dry completely. See Figure 7-22 for a completed view.

❻ Remove the tape covering the rope border. Apply tape along the outside edges of the border and burnish well. Using the flat artist's brush and acrylic paints, apply an S-shape 1/4" in from the corner, starting from the upper right on the tape and moving down to lower left. Paint the shapes one after the other in a sequence of blue, green, and mauve as shown in Figure 7-23.

Continue painting S-shapes until you reach the corner.

7-23

❼ Curve the S-shapes around the corner (Figure 7-24) and continue painting the remaining three sides until complete.

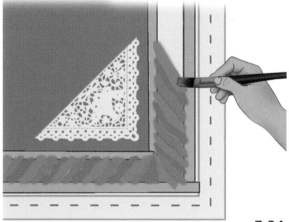

7-24

❽ Follow the instructions in Chapter 3 for Sealing Your Floorcloth and Hemming the Edges.

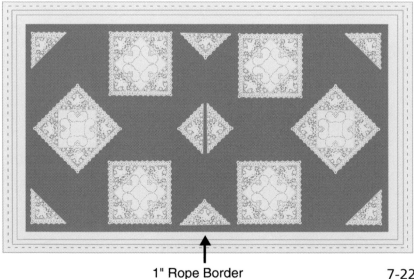

1" Rope Border

7-22

CHAPTER 8:
ADVANCED
FLOORCLOTH
PROJECTS

Use your skills and experience to master the exceptional projects in this chapter. The level of difficulty is increased, designs are more complex, and additional working time is necessary. Many of the same techniques are used but in different combinations and more intricate patterns.

Choose from projects such as stained glass, wallpaper and fringe, fabric appliquéd animals, or a Southwestern theme. As always, patience is the key to completing the projects successfully, so work slowly and carefully and you will be rewarded with a unique floor covering and an extraordinary piece of art.

STAINED GLASS

Step into a pool of light with this distinctive stained glass floorcloth. Create this subtle mixture of pattern and color using several shades of colored pencils, puzzle painting, and a silver paint pen to simulate the leading. Alternative methods for applying the color are sponging, stenciling, or hand-painting with acrylic paints. This floorcloth should be made on a square piece of medium-weight primed canvas, such as #569 Dallas, to simplify stretching and hemming.

Finished size: 36" round
Technique: puzzle painting, outlining, hand shading

TECHNIQUE

❶ Stretch the canvas on a flat frame or open stretcher, following the instructions in Chapter 3.

❷ Apply one uneven coat of ivory paint to create a shaded effect. Let dry.

❸ Using the template provided, enlarge the design on a copy machine or graph paper as discussed in Chapter 3, to the size of 36" in diameter (some copy stores have the capability to enlarge drawings to 36" on one page). Transfer the design to the canvas with carbon paper, graphite paper, or graphite shading (Figure 8-1).

8-1

❹ Refer to Figure 8-2 and shade the solid areas with colored pencil according to the color-coded letter key. Shade the outer edges

of each shape (closest to the leading) darker than the center to simulate the colored glass.

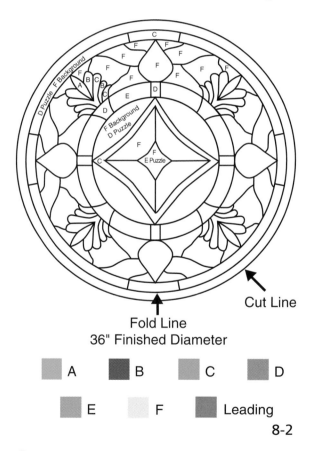

Cut Line

Fold Line
36" Finished Diameter

	A		B		C		D
	E		F		Leading		

8-2

❺ Using olive green and blue markers, fill in the designated areas with the Puzzle Painting technique as explained on page 30 (Figure 8-3).

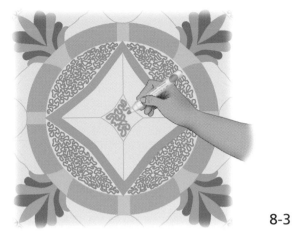

8-3

6 Apply the leading with the silver paint pen along all the pencil lines (Figure 8-4). Let dry. Spray the entire canvas with artist's fixative to prevent smudging.

8-4

7 Follow the instructions in Chapter 3 for Sealing Your Floorcloth and Hemming the Edges.

Decorative puzzle painting lends color, pattern, and texture to this otherwise ordinary stained glass design.

STAINED GLASS TEMPLATE

ANIMAL ESCAPADES

Keep safe through the night with your friends from the jungle. Make this wonderful children's floorcloth using fabric animals and treetops, paper tree trunks, and a painted moon—all surrounded by a charming rhyme. Other methods of embellishment are hand-painting, stenciling, stamping, or a combination of all three techniques.

Finished size: 42" x 28"
Technique: paper decoupage, fabric appliqué, hand-painting

(Fabric used: Animals - #1179B "In the Beginning" courtesy of Alexander Henry Fabrics, Treetops - #9147, Hunter, courtesy of Hoffman Fabrics)

MATERIALS

- *Canvas 46" x 32"*
- *Stretchers*
- *Fabric:*
  animals—3/4 yd. (I used Alexander Henry Fabrics, Inc. #1179B In the Beginning)
  treetops—1/2 yd. (I used Hoffman California International Fabrics, #9147 Hunter)
  tree trunks—1 package brown or gold paper napkins or tissue paper
- *Paint:*
  background—blue exterior latex house paint to match the blue background color of the fabric
  designs—acrylic paints in yellow, forest green
- *Brushes:*
  1" sponge paint brush

4" sponge paint brush or roller medium round artist's brush
- *Metallic gold paint pen*
- *Ruler*
- *White pencil*
- *Painter's masking tape*
- *Mod Podge glue*
- *Plastic putty knife*
- *Scissors*
- *Paper towels*
- *Craft knife*
- *Straight pins*
- *No-fray glue*
- *Disappearing marking pen*
- *Rubber cement or hot glue gun for hemming*
- *1 qt. water-based acrylic sealer, varnish, or polyurethane in matte or satin finish*

Colors shown in photo:
Designs: DecoArt Americana acrylics in Moon Yellow DA7, Forest Green DA50

Cut Size 46" x 32"
Finished Size 42" x 28"

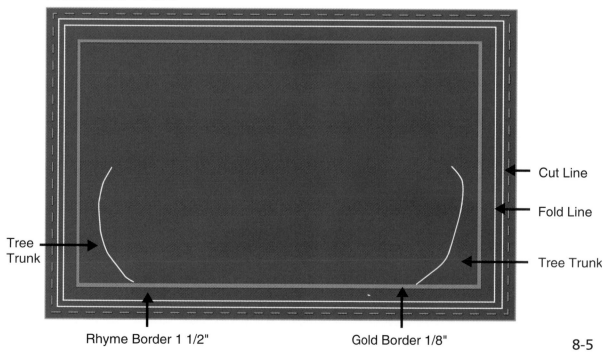

Tree Trunk

Cut Line

Fold Line

Tree Trunk

Rhyme Border 1 1/2"

Gold Border 1/8"

8-5

TECHNIQUE

1 Stretch the canvas on a flat or open frame, following the instructions in Chapter 3.

2 Apply two coats of blue background color to the entire canvas with a 4" sponge brush or roller.

3 Refer to Figure 8-5 and use a white pencil to draw in the cut line, fold line, 1½" border, and tree trunks. Use the gold paint pen to apply a 1/8" line along the border drawn 1½" in from the edge.

4 Cut the animal fabric apart into pieces approximately 6". Sparingly apply no-fray glue to all fabric edges (Figure 8-6). Any background trimmed away can be filled in between the fabric pieces with forest green paint to simulate the fabric background.

8-6

5 Arrange the fabric pieces to fit between the trees. Label the back of each piece with a piece of masking tape (a, b, c). Sketch a diagram on the canvas as a placement guide for the pieces (Figure 8-7).

6 Fold the treetop fabric right sides together. Using a disappearing marker or white pencil, draw the treetop shapes on the fabric using the project photo as a guide. Place several straight pins inside each shape to hold the fabric in place (Figure 8-8).

8-7

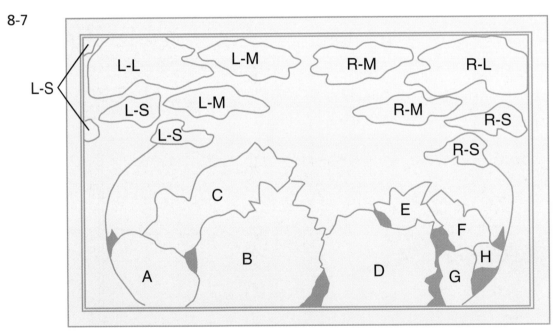

Solid areas to be painted green

L — Left Leaves   R — Right Leaves   S Small, M Medium, L Large

A — Giraffes & Rams
B — Cats, Ducks, Zebras, Tigers & Birds
C — Noah's Ark, Cows, Giraffes & Elephants
D — Zebras, Ducks, Cats, Monkeys & Rabbits

E — Birds & Tigers
F — Giraffes
G — Rams
H — Elephants

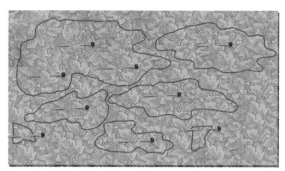
8-8

7 Cut out the fabric leaf tops with a pair of scissors, remove the pins, and apply no-fray glue to all the fabric edges. Label each piece with masking tape to note its size and placement—large, medium, or small left tree; or large, medium, or small right tree (Figure 8-9). Add these labels to the diagram drawn with the animal fabric.

8-9

8 Position the animal and treetop fabric pieces on the canvas and trace around the outside edges with white pencil. Draw in the moon placement above the animals and pencil in the tree branches with white pencil, connecting the trunk and leaf motifs together. Place an "x" in the areas between the fabric animals that require green background paint to match the background of the fabric (Figure 8-10).

9 Remove the animal fabric and apply forest green paint to the areas marked with an "x" (Figure 8-11). Use a 1" sponge brush to apply yellow on the moon and finish the edges with the medium round artist's brush.

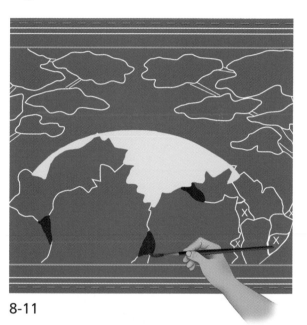
8-11

8-10

10 Apply tape along the edges of the tree trunk and branches. Trim the tape to fit with a craft knife and burnish well with a craft stick or putty knife. Glue the paper napkins inside the tape following the Paper Napkin instructions on page 53 (Figure 8-12).

12 Using a gold paint pen, write the following rhyme in the outside border (Figure 8-14): "Lions here, tigers there, giraffes and monkeys everywhere. Moonlight shines strong and bright. Keeps us safe till daylight."

8-14

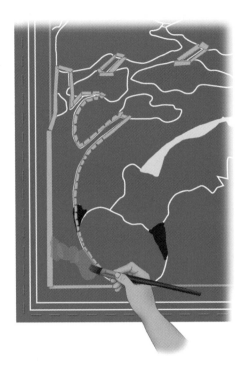

8-12

13 Follow the instructions in Chapter 3 for Sealing Your Floorcloth and Hemming the Edges.

11 Glue the fabric appliqués in position on the canvas, carefully burnishing each to remove any air bubbles and excess glue (Figure 8-13). Refer to the Fabric Appliqué instructions on page 55 for detailed information.

8-13

LATTICE & FRINGE

The lattice motif has endured through hundreds of years and many styles of decorating. Its popularity is attributed to its design versatility and ability to coordinate a variety of patterns and textures together into one working design. Here it is paired with an impressive wallpaper border and tri-colored fringe to create a quiet but sophisticated traditional floorcloth.

Finished size: 55" x 32"
Technique: paper decoupage, freehand lattice, faux fringe

(Wallpaper border #JH8053B courtesy of Imperial Wallcoverings)

MATERIALS

- *Canvas 59" x 36"*
- *Stretchers*
- *Wallpaper border (I used Imperial Wallcoverings, Inc. #JH 8053B)*
- *Paint:*
  background—taupe exterior latex house paint to match the taupe in the wallpaper border
  designs—acrylics in off-white, burgundy, green, metallic gold
- *Metallic gold paint pen or marker*
- *Brushes:*
  medium round artist's brush
  small round artist's brush
  2 4" sponge brushes
- *Wallpaper adhesive or Mod Podge*
- *Ruler*
- *Craft knife*
- *Craft stick or plastic putty knife for burnishing*
- *Palette*
- *Paper towels*
- *Pencil*
- *Rubber cement or hot glue gun for hemming.*
- *1 qt. water-based acrylic sealer, varnish, or polyurethane in matte or satin finish*

Colors shown in photo:
Background: Benjamin Moore MooreGard latex house paint #1024
Designs: DecoArt Americana acrylics in Buttermilk DA3, Deep Burgundy DA128, Green Mist DA177, and DecoArt Dazzling Metallics Glorious Gold DA71

TECHNIQUE

❶ Stretch the canvas on a flat or open stretcher, following the instructions in Chapter 3.

❷ Using a 4" sponge brush or roller, apply two coats of background color. Let dry between coats.

❸ Refer to Figure 8-15 and pencil in the cut line, fold line, and top and bottom knot lines.

Cut Size 59" x 36"
Finished Size 55" x 32" including fringe

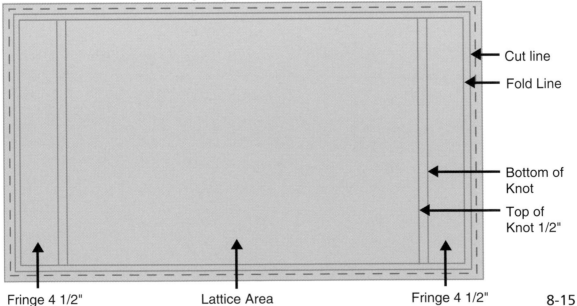

Cut line

Fold Line

Bottom of Knot

Top of Knot 1/2"

Fringe 4 1/2"   Lattice Area   Fringe 4 1/2"   8-15

4 Divide the top to bottom lattice area by three and mark it. Divide the left to right lattice area by four and mark it. Using a pencil, connect the guide marks with diagonal lines, forming the latticework (Figure 8-16).

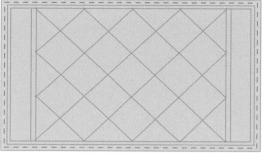

8-16

5 Follow the Lattice instructions on page 28 in Chapter 4 to apply the lattice design in the center rectangle of the floorcloth.

6 Pencil a wallpaper gluing guideline 1" in from the outside edge of the lattice section, and another 6⅜" from that (Figure 8-17).

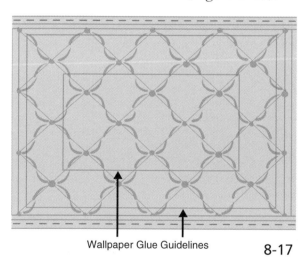

Wallpaper Glue Guidelines

8-17

7 Cut four pieces of wallpaper border—two lengths plus 1", and two widths plus 1" for overlapping and mitering the corners. On this particular wallpaper, I trimmed the bottom taupe border off with a craft knife and straight edge.

8 Use a 2" sponge brush to apply glue to the first 6"-8" of the back of one length of wallpaper and to the corresponding area on the canvas (Figures 8-18 and 8-19).

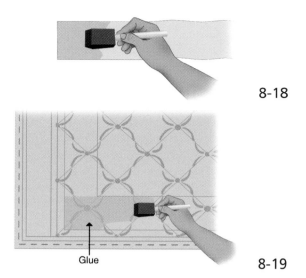

8-18

Glue

8-19

9 Place the wallpaper piece between the guidelines, overlapping the corner about 1/2". Use a plastic putty knife to smooth the paper, moving from the center to the outside edges to remove excess glue and air bubbles (Figure 8-20).

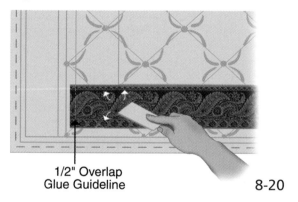

1/2" Overlap
Glue Guideline

8-20

10 Trim the excess paper from the corner with a craft knife by aligning a straight edge with the guideline (Figure 8-21). Burnish the paper again. Continue gluing 6"-8" sections of wallpaper along the guideline to the end. Burnish and trim the corner in the same manner.

8-21

11 Turn the corner and glue the next piece of wallpaper, overlapping the corner edge as you did in Step 10. Instead of trimming the excess paper straight along the guideline, miter the corner by aligning the straight edge with the inside corner and the outside corner. Carefully cut the excess paper away with a craft knife (Figures 8-22 and 8-22 detail). Continue applying glue and smoothing the paper in sections until all the pieces are glued and the border is complete.

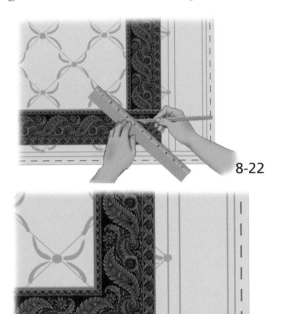

8-22

8-22 detail

12 To add the fringe, draw four or five circles and bell shapes inside the knot guidelines (Figure 8-23).

8-23

13 Mix one or two drops of off-white with some burgundy paint in a small mixing cup and thin with a little water. Use the medium round

artist's brush to fill in the first knot. To paint the fringe, start at the meeting point of the knot and the bell. Pull the brush down to the bottom of the bell, overlapping some brush strokes on the ones beside it. This will create a streaked effect to simulate the yarns of actual fringe. Continue painting one knot and one bell shape at a time (Figure 8-24). Let dry.

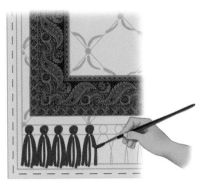

Darkest Color First   8-24

14 Use the small round brush to apply green paint to only the center area of each knot and bell shape in the same manner as Step 13 (Figure 8-25). Let dry

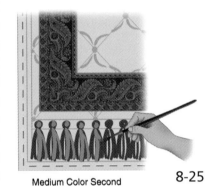

Medium Color Second   8-25

15 Mix several drops of water with metallic gold to make a wash. With the small round brush, very lightly apply the color to the center of each knot and fringe (Figure 8-26).

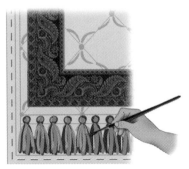

Highlight Color Last   8-26

16 Follow the instructions in Chapter 3 for Sealing Your Floorcloth and Hemming the Edges.

SANTA FE

Southwestern design has always conveyed its own sense of style and sophistication. Color, pattern, and texture create an aged but refined piece of history. This project combines paper decoupage, stamping, and taping techniques to simplify a project that would otherwise be extremely difficult and time consuming. The large red motifs, circles, and center triangles are paper decoupage. This saves you from painstakingly taping off all the angles and curves. The border triangles and central arrows are created with stamps quickly and easily. You may choose to make color copies from the color templates provided or paint your own using the black and white template. Make the color copies and take one with you to match when purchasing the paint. The floorcloth is completed with an addition of fiber lines to enhance the aged feeling.

Finished size: 40" x 26¾"
Technique: paper decoupage, stamping, taping, color washing

∾ *Canvas 44" x 31"*
∾ *Stretchers*
∾ *Paint:*
   background—medium taupe or
      sand color exterior latex paint
Note: If painting your own designs,
you'll need acrylic paints in blue,
teal green, and red to match the
color copies.
∾ *Required copies as shown on*
   templates
∾ *Thick foam or expandable*
   sponges for stamps
∾ *Brushes:*
   2" sponge brush
   4" sponge brush
   1/2" flat artist's brush
∾ *Mod Podge or wallpaper*
   adhesive
∾ *Fine black permanent marker*

∾ *Light brown colored pencil*
∾ *Ruler*
∾ *Painter's masking tape*
∾ *Craft knife*
∾ *Craft stick or plastic putty knife*
   for burnishing
∾ *Ballpoint pen*
∾ *Pencil*
∾ *Paper towels*
∾ *Rubber cement or hot glue gun*
   for hemming
∾ *1 qt. water-based acrylic sealer,*
   varnish, or polyurethane in
   matte or satin finish
∾ *Fixative spray for markers that*
   are not permanent

Colors shown in photo:
Background: Benjamin Moore MooreGard exterior latex house paint #957
Designs (if not using color copies): DecoArt Americana acrylics in Blueberry DA37, Teal Green DA107, Primary Red (Naphol Crimson) DA199

TECHNIQUE

❶ Stretch the canvas on a flat frame or open stretcher, following the instructions in Chapter 3.

❷ Haphazardly apply one coat of background color to the canvas using a sponge brush, covering some areas lightly and other areas more heavily. This will create an uneven, somewhat aged appearance. Let dry.

❸ Refer to Figure 8-27 and pencil in the cut line, fold line, red, blue, and green outside borders, and the center of the floorcloth.

Cut Size 44" x 31"
Finished Size 40" x 26 3/4"

Center

Cut Line

Fold Line

3/4" Green
Border

1 1/4" Red
Border

5/8" Blue
Border

8-27

❹ Cover the red border area and the outside of the blue and green border area with painter's masking tape, burnishing the edges well. Use the 2" sponge brush to paint the blue and green borders, applying one streaky coat instead of two. This will give the paint an aged appearance (Figure 8-28). When the paint is tacky, remove the tape and let dry thoroughly. Repeat for the red border if painting the motifs yourself. Paint one sheet of white paper blue and one sheet green.

8-28

❺ You have two options for creating the large red motifs, center circles, and triangles. **Option #1:** Cut around the large red motif to separate it from the other templates. Make five color copies, enlarging the motif to 7". Make five copies of the remaining circle and triangle templates at the original size (four are required but it's a good idea to have one extra).

Option #2: Paint five sheets of white paper red, transfer the design onto four of the sheets and trim with a craft knife and ruler (Figure 8-29). To transfer the design, refer to Enlarging and Transferring the Design on page 19. Repeat for the circles and triangles.

8-29

❻ Cut out the number of shapes needed and label each on the back with its size and placement.

❼ Refer to the Decoupage Cutout instructions on page 49 for gluing the paper motifs to the canvas. Glue the 1⅝" blue circle in the center of the canvas and the large and small green and red triangles beside it. See Figure 8-30 for placement measurements and Figure 8-31 for application. When the blue circle is dry, glue the 1/2" red circle inside it.

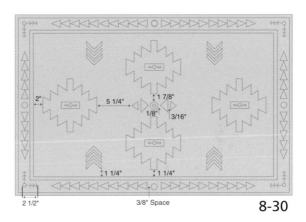

8-30

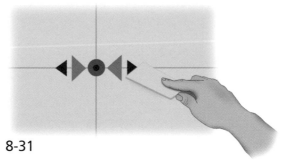

8-31

❽ With the 2" sponge brush, apply Mod Podge glue or wallpaper adhesive to half of the back of one large red paper motif (Figure 8-32). Place it in position and burnish it well with a plastic putty knife (Figure 8-33). Wipe away any excess glue with a paper towel. Fold back the remaining half of the paper and apply glue to the canvas underneath. Carefully press the remaining half of the paper in place and burnish. Repeat with the three remaining red motifs.

8-32

8-33

9 Glue and burnish the 13/16" blue circles in the center of the red border on all four sides. Glue and burnish the 5/8" green corner circles. Let dry. Using a thin permanent black marker, draw arrows on either side of the green corner circles and inside the large red motifs (Figure 8-34). Let dry. Center, glue, and burnish the 7/16" green circles inside the center large red motif over the black arrows.

8-34

10 Trace the arrow template on a piece of rubber, foam, or sponge and cut with a craft or utility knife. Apply blue paint to the printing side of the stamp and place it in location on the canvas. Refer to the Stamping instructions on page 37 for detailed instructions. Stamp all the interior blue arrows and clean the stamp with a baby wipe. Stamp all the green arrows, clean the stamp, and stamp the remaining outside blue arrows (Figure 8-35).

8-35

11 Repeat Step 10 for the ivory border triangle stamp in the red border area (Figure 8-36).

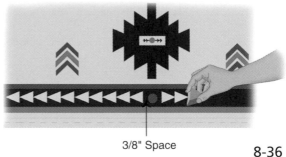

3/8" Space

8-36

12 Using a light brown colored pencil, draw long horizontal wavy lines or streaks randomly throughout the width of the floorcloth (Figure 8-37). This will enhance the aged appearance of the background and add texture similar to woven cloth.

8-37

13 Follow the instructions in Chapter 3 for Sealing Your Floorcloth and Hemming the Edges.

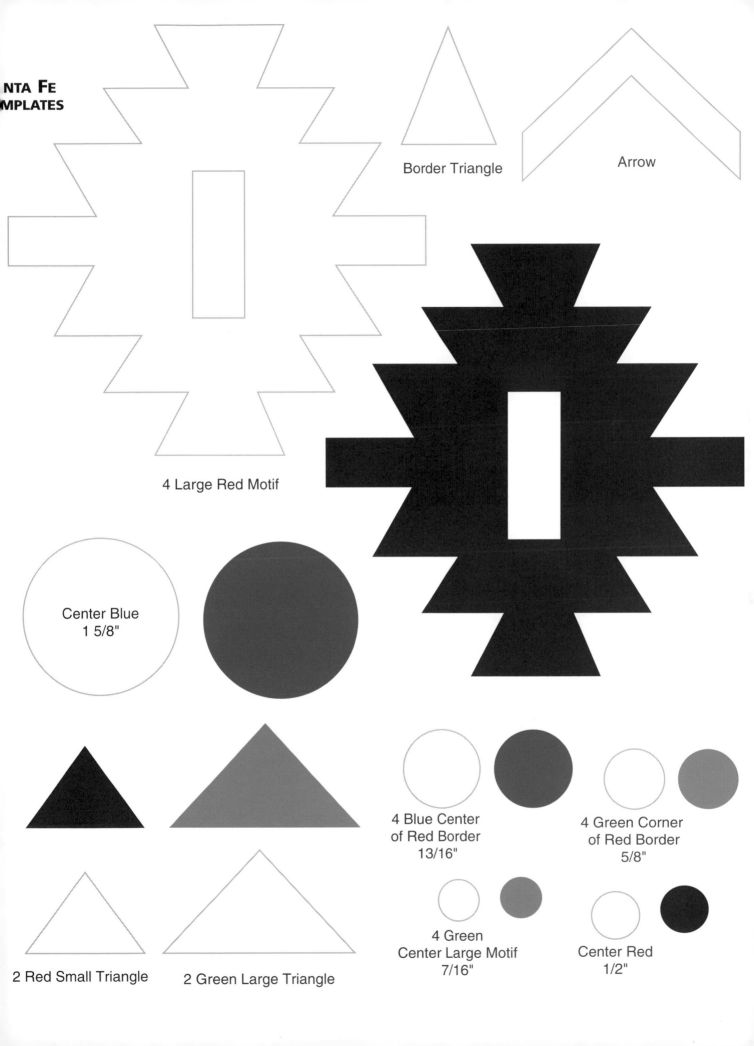

NTA FE
MPLATES

Border Triangle

Arrow

4 Large Red Motif

Center Blue
1 5/8"

4 Blue Center
of Red Border
13/16"

4 Green Corner
of Red Border
5/8"

4 Green
Center Large Motif
7/16"

Center Red
1/2"

2 Red Small Triangle

2 Green Large Triangle

Caroline O'Neill Kuchinsky is an artistic designer well known in the Washington, D.C. metropolitan area. After receiving a degree in Interior Design she built a design firm specializing in custom-designed canvas floorcloths, fiber art carpets, and a variety of unique home decorating accessories. An integral part of her business and career has been the development of a series of workshops including *Canvas Floorcloths*, *Advanced Floorcloth Techniques*, *Faux Painting*, and *Home Decorating on a Budget*. The workshops and seminars have been conducted through the Smithsonian Institution, Maryland's Montpelier Mansion, continuing education programs, and privately through her design firm.

Caroline's business and many workshops and seminars have been featured in newspaper articles in *The Washington Post Home Section*, *The Washington Post Magazine,* and other local Washington newspapers.

GENERAL ART SUPPLIES & CANVAS

Ameratex
(800) 225-7890
2861 West Franklin St.
Baltimore, MD 21223
Canvas (wholesale)

Baltimore Canvas Products
(800) 225-2391 or (410) 947-7890
2861 West Franklin St.
Baltimore, MD 21223
Canvas (retail)

Benjamin Moore & Co.
(800) 344-0400
51 Chestnut Ridge Road
Montvale, NJ 07645
Interior/exterior paints and varnishes, glazes, stains

Burns Paint & Equipment
(512) 227-9353
900 Broadway
San Antonio, TX 78215
Japan paints

Dick Blick Art Materials
(800) 723-2787
P.O. Box 26
Allentown, PA 18105
General art supplies

Hamilton Brush
P.O. Box 5176
Westport, CT 06881
Paint brushes

Jerry's Artarama
(800) 827-8478
P.O. Box 58638
Raleigh, NC 27658
Art supplies and canvas

Nasco
(800) 447-8192
P.O. Box 1267
Galesburg, IL 61402
Art supplies

S. Wolf's Sons
771 9th Avenue
New York, NY 10019
Complete range of art supplies

Torrington Brush Works, Inc.
(800) 262-7874
63 Avenue "A"
P.O. Box 56
Torrington, CT 06790
Extensive range of specialty brushes

SELECTED READING

Cooper, Kathy and Hersey, Jan. *The Complete Book of Floorcloths*, North Carolina, Lark Books. 1997

Decker, Peggy. *Painted Floor Cloths*, Georgia, Plaid Enterprises. 1991

Drucker, Mindy and Finkelstein, Pierre. *Recipes For Surfaces*, New York, Simon and Schuster Inc. 1993

Everett, Avis. *Simply Stenciled Floorcloths*, Georgia, Plaid Enterprises. 1993

Gaus, Jane. *Stenciled Floor Cloths*, Georgia, Plaid Enterprises. 1994

Home Decorating Institute, The. *Decorative Painting*, Minnesota, Cy DeCosse. 1994.

Marx, Ina Brousseau and Marx, Allen and Marx, Robert. *Professional Painted Finishes*, New York, Watson-Guptill Publications. 1991

INDEX

adhesive 13, 23
Animal Escapades 104
appliqué, fabric 15, 55, 73, 104
basecoating 18
border lines 18
borders 31, 73
bricks 39
brushes 13
canvas 11
caring for floorcloths 26
Circle of Stars 66
Classical Table Runner 79
color scheme 6
color washing 44, 113
Contemporary Crescents 70
crescent painting 29, 70
cut line 18
cutting canvas 17
decoupage, paper . . . .
. . . . 15, 48, 64, 66, 79, 87, 92, 104, 109, 113
    borders 51
    cutouts 49
design 5
doily spray 40, 96
enlarging designs 19
faux finish 41
feathers 14
ferns 40
fold line 18
frames 12
freehand painting 28
fringe 34, 109
Fruits & Flowers 73
Garden View 84
glaze 44
hemming 22, 25
hot glue 23
lattice 28, 109
Lattice & Fringe 109
Ornamental Tile 60
outlining 100
paint 15
paint brushes 13
paper napkins 53
patterns 8
preparing canvas 18
primer 11, 12

Projects
    Animal Escapades 104
    Circle of Stars 66
    Classical Table Runner 79
    Contemporary Crescents 70
    Fruits & Flowers 73
    Garden View 84
    Lattice & Fringe 109
    Ornamental Tile 60
    Rainbow Hopscotch 76
    Santa Fe 113
    Stained Glass 100
    Swirls, Curls & Waves 64
    Victorian Lace 96
    Welcome Home 92
    White & Black Marble 88
puzzle painting 30, 100
Rainbow Hopscotch 76
reducing designs 19
roping 35, 96
rubber backing 13
rubber cement 23
samples 8
sandpaper 14
Santa Fe 113
sealer 12, 21
sponge brushes 14
sponging 42, 84
Stained Glass 100
stamping 14, 37, 84, 113
stenciling 14, 36, 92
stretchers 11, 12, 17
stretching canvas 17
swirls, curls & waves 31, 64, 68
taping 32, 64, 66, 76, 79, 92, 113
textures 8
tissue paper 53
tools 11, 13
transferring designs 20
varnish 11
veining 44, 87
Victorian Lace 96
wax 11
Welcome Home 92
White & Black Marble 88

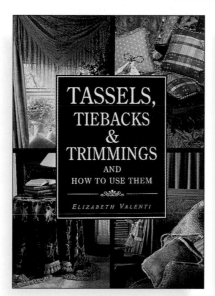
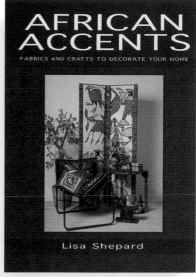
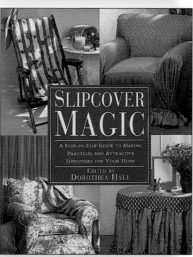